why dance matters

yale

university

press

new haven

and

london

mindy

aloff

why

dance

matters

"Why X Matters" is a registered trademark of Yale
University.

Yale University Press books may be purchased in
quantity for educational, business, or promotional use.
For information, please e-mail sales.press@yale.edu
(U.S. office) or sales@yaleup.co.uk (U.K. office).

Set in Times Roman and Adobe Garamond type by
Integrated Publishing Solutions.
Printed in the United States of America.

ISBN 978-0-300-20452-0 (hardcover : alk. paper)
Library of Congress Control Number: 2022934244
A catalogue record for this book is available from the
British Library.

This paper meets the requirements of ANSI/NISO
Z39.48-1992 (Permanence of Paper).

10 9 8 7 6 5 4 3 2 1

contents

why dance matters

I

child's play

On the facing page of this book is a mysterious, even mesmerizing photograph of two children in the middle of an otherwise empty New York street in 1940, possibly in high summer given their light clothing. The location may well have been East Harlem, where the photographer herself lived, and which, at that time, was a neighborhood populated by families with a variety of back-grounds, including Italian Americans and African Americans. New Yorkers who knew the city in the years leading up to World War II will tell you that working-class children, as the ones here look to have been, spent a lot of

[*Children Dancing*] *N.Y.*, Helen Levitt, circa 1940 (© Film Documents LLC, courtesy Galerie Thomas Zander, Cologne)

time outdoors, absent adult supervision, especially in the warmer months. Air conditioners before the war were few and far between; one left the house after breakfast and often didn't return for hours, maybe not until dinnertime.

Even if one's pockets were empty, there was lots on the street to keep a child occupied. Helen Levitt, one of the most perceptive street photographers of city children in the twentieth century, recorded many pastimes. The caption for this image reads that the children are dancing. Now, for viewers interested in photography, that identification will be of secondary interest. For if you are interested in photography, you are going to fix immediately on the contrast of bright light and deep shadow—a contrast that Levitt caught with particular bravura in the alternating tones of the little girl's skin against her grayscale sock then the strap of her blazing white Mary Jane shoe. Eventually, one notices that, by some miracle, the girl has managed to dance on the very edge between sunlight and the overhanging shadow of a nearby building whose presence is visible only through its shadow—increasingly dark, it seems, the longer one looks at it. And facing the girl and entirely swaddled in the shadow, is the other child, a boy.

That's the aesthetics of the image, photographically speaking. Some observers may begin to make associations, working from the aesthetics into something more alarming. It just seems to happen that the girl's fair skin looks as brilliant in the light as the white collar and waistband of her dress. And it just seems to happen that the boy's African American skin seems to grow increasingly dark, inky at his hair and what appear to be long black socks under his camper shorts. From there, a few observers may even push forward into a kind of vision of the races, equating sunlight with good fortune and shadow with looming unfairness or tragedy. Suddenly, the picture takes on a layer of social commentary of which the children are unaware—a layer comprehended (and, it might be argued, to some extent curated) by the photographer and those of us who join in recognizing it.

I've known this photograph for several decades, but I never looked at it this way until recently, when the light-and-shadow implications were explained to me by Marvin Hoshino, professor emeritus of photography at Queens College and the co-executor of Levitt's estate (and now, lamentably, no longer alive). Until I spoke with Marvin, all I saw in the image was the dancing. To me, the picture remains astonishing in that the movement of the children alone tells us what they are doing. The scene gives a viewer no costumes, no accompanying musicians, no theatrical or studio or ballroom surround to provide a clue that they dance. And even the movement itself is unusual for a dance picture, since neither dancer is depicted in the middle of shifting bodily weight from one foot to another: neither is seen to be taking a step. Nevertheless, if the caption were missing, one would still guess that dancing is what they do. They are caught moving in a way that has no practical purpose yet is clearly expressive in purely physical terms and that is also intentionally a display of a special way to address one another in the moment—movement for its own sake, exaggerated for the pleasure of the mover and, secondarily, the mover's addressee, or audience. The achievement of what they do is entirely a matter of how they do it.

The fact that the children are choosing their actions—that is, serving as improvisers of both their choreography and its execution—gives the image an especially joyous element of play. And yet, it is also unquestionable that, in improvising, they are calling on memories of having seen other dancers, perhaps professional dancers, enact steps or phrases that serve as models. The improvisation is not invention, although, in the right context and with the right experience, it can lead to invention.

Is it possible to figure out what kind of dancing they have in mind to imitate?

My own guess is that they are aiming to mimic classical ballet. Actually, it looks to me as if they are partly trying to reproduce a bit of ballet in earnest and, at the same time, playing at earnestly reproducing it. The girl could be trying for one of a couple of things. Perhaps she is anchoring herself with her left foot en route to trying to point it—and maybe even lift it a little—in a classical tendu that will become an arabesque. Or, perhaps she is doing her best to put her legs into ballet's fifth position, which, if she knew the logistics of how to manage it, would result in her feet placed instep to instep and toe to heel. Given the fact that her upper body is putting her on track to move forward, I think that the first option is more likely; yet ballet is a tricky practice, and the surprise of which foot moves where from fifth position is a major aspect of the technique. For her purposes, though, the girl doesn't have to get whatever foot position she tries for exactly right; she only has to get it right enough, for her real motivation is gesture, and hers is extraordinary, eloquent—a sculpture into which her full attention (one might say her full being) is invested. The carriage of the girl's upper body and the dynamism of her arms, the fantastical position of her fingers, the intensity of her gaze—these bespeak Western theatrical dancing in general and ballet in particular.

We turn to the boy. Of the two children, he is the one whose face radiates delight, even joy. His personal emotion reads as the emotion of the entire picture. At the same time, though, his body is not fully committed to the movement he has chosen to perform. His feet are in motion, the right foot slightly lifted so that his weight is on his left leg. Yet, unlike the girl, he is not trying to perfect the position of his feet, which are side by side and more or less parallel. And he, also, may be trying for one of a couple of possibilities. Perhaps he is attempting to pose with his right arm high and rounded and his left arm held to the side. If his left arm were fully waist-high, he would be assuming a carriage of the arms frequent in classical dancing. Or perhaps he is taking the cartoonish position one sometimes finds in ballet satire, with the dancer partnering himself in an approximation of a ballerina figurine turning in a 360-degree pirouette on a music box. And in contrast to the girl's open-hearted energy, the boy's hands are retracted, the fingers curled softly, as he seems curled inward with his own thoughts, enjoying a joke that he alone has heard.

Finally, the children's social attitudes toward each other lead them in different directions. She dances in his presence but only secondarily *for* him, whereas he dances for her. One feels that her satisfaction is in the dance, which permits her to relate to him by bestowing her performance on his vision, while his satisfaction is in the connection dance gives him to her. They are not dancing in sync; their playfulness appears to originate in different psychic places. Each child does something unique; each is the star of her or his own private stage: they are thoroughly, adorably, irrepressibly children. And yet, at least for the space of the photograph, they are incipient artists, too.

It seems impossible that they would have invented those movements. Did they see some dancers practicing outdoors, perhaps in East Harlem? Did they see a movie with ballet dancers in it, or a newsreel, or a performance at their elementary school? For what they are doing is what the very greatest of adult dancers also do: they are attempting to reproduce a model, an example (in this case, an example they are remembering), and, in reproducing it, to speak the language in a personal way, according to what the proportions and flexibility of the body can manage as they impel it—at once consciously and intuitively—in service of the mental image they aim for.

Many readers will connect with these children of long ago. For my own part, I'm guessing what they might have felt because, when I was five, my mother enrolled me in classes in a balletic interpretive style, with a teacher named Ursula Melita, a refugee from Nazi Germany. As the founder of Ballet des Jeunes, a company of children, Miss Melita did not ask her students simply to pretend to be flowers; in her class, we *were* flowers. Regardless of our ages, she required commitment to the dance and to the creative imagination. My mother liked Miss Melita's loyalty to her art, and to keep my interest going between the weekly sessions, Mom bought me a little book of beguiling photographs, on silky coated paper, that showed members of the Sadler's Wells Ballet in poses of astonishing beauty and strength, many of them hauntingly lit. (Years later, I discovered that those haunting studio photographs were by Gordon Anthony.) I pored over and over that treasury, trying to memorize those images both for their own magnificence and for the practical purpose of using them as guides in Miss Melita's classes. I remember an assignment to be a snowman (a snowperson in today's parlance). It was up to us how to become that creature. At first the assignment seemed impossible. But then I attacked it the way I've attacked almost all impossible assignments since: I broke it down to smaller, specific steps. Snowfolks are round, roly-poly, I figured; and so I lay down and rolled around on the floor. Connection in my head was a little vague between my snowperson and the book's vision of, say, Svetlana Beriosova, in a white classical-length tutu, posed in what I later learned was an arabesque allongée; however, I trusted that there *was* a connection, and that when I got to one of the older girls' classes I'd learn exactly what it was. My trust in the logic particular to dancing—the logic of body and mind implicit in the physical linkings between this step and that gesture, this gesture and that pose—was for me from the beginning the basis of the magic of dance. It still is.

Regardless of how simplistic my own solution to the dance assignment was, the process of association by which I arrived at it is essential to dance improvisers and choreographers in all traditions and practices. It relates to an aspect of how human beings put together ideas and experience, how we remember, visualize, experiment, and plan. Miss Melita knew that and encouraged it, even in her classes for five-year-olds. I believe it was those classes that first revealed to me the secret of why dance matters on a personal level: for the dancer, the act of dancing is an immediate projection, often faster than conscious thought, of one's interior being. On the most fundamental level, dancing unites emotion with perception, anticipation, stored imagery, and the realization of them together in time and space by way of one's own body. When to dance is to embody an ideal—dancing as the epitome of personal freedom, in choreography whose constraints both challenge and encourage that freedom—the result can be a feeling of wholeness in the observer as well as in the dancer, even when the subject of the choreography is dark.

For the dancer, professional or amateur, the benefits of dancing for the body certainly help to explain why so many people move rhythmically to music for the sake of moving that way— that is, why so many people dance—at least in the years of their lives when they feel good. When they don't feel good, many also seek out dancing to bring them at least momentarily to something like health. The use of modified elements of dance training today helps sufferers from respiratory ailments, Parkinson's disease, deterioration of the muscles and memory during the process of aging, and other conditions. And stories are legion of small children and young adults (some of whom grow into heralded professional dancers) being advised by physicians to study ballet in order to strengthen the feet or the back. One such young adult was Marian Chace, who had injured her back in a diving accident. In 1923, around the age of twenty-seven, she took her doctor's suggestion and, in an effort to heal herself, began to study modern dance at the Denishawn School in New York City. Chace went on to found her own small dance company, to choreograph, and to philosophize about movement. Even so, she is remembered primarily because she veered away from performing. In the course of experimenting with dance movement and encountering the practice of psychodrama in work she did with traumatized GIs at the Washington [D.C.] School of Psychiatry during World War II—work in which she helped those damaged by trauma to use movement as communication—she gave up her theatrical ambitions so she could concentrate on bringing what we now call dance therapy to individuals who do not want to become performers but for whom aspects of dance are therapeutic. Chace and her colleagues in the practice of dance therapy showed that dancing was useful off the stage not only for muscles and bones but also for, if not the restoration, at least the improvement of mental health.

A quarter century after Helen Levitt took that photograph in 1940 of children dancing, I graduated from the Philadelphia High School for Girls, a single-sex, academically focused public high school. (Boys who were academically driven attended the all-boys' Central High.) My mother taught at another single-sex public high school in Philadelphia, the William Penn High School for Girls. However, seeing what a toll it took on her not only to teach her students but also to serve as a de facto nurse, counselor, and social worker to help them get through very harsh home lives, I then had no desire to follow in her footsteps as a teacher. I was good at math, and since my father was an engineer, I hazily expected to go into something along that line.

Like a tornado out of a clear blue sky, dancing came along and derailed my vague expectations. At the end of junior high, my string-bean body transformed itself into the shape of an eggplant, with attendant changes in gait and coordination. My folks wondered if I might enjoy a renewed acquaintance with ballet—Miss Melita's classes having long been abandoned for schoolwork—and I began to study classical dancing in earnest: without warning, I fell deeply in love with the comfortingly structured, excitingly musical, physically and psychically challenging experience of taking a ballet class. It was as if I'd been dropped into a hole in the earth and emerged, gasping yet flooded with life, in a brand-new world.

It was a classic mismatch. My own inherited physique—wide where ballet needs narrow, flesh where the art prefers bone—might be useful for harsh Slavic winters or for bearing enough children to carry forward the family name in periods of high infant mortality. However, it was not built to sustain the secret level of abstract design, the Euclidean geometry, that renders classical dancing "classical." My sportswoman's initiative to try to jump as high and land as softly as any of the teenaged boys in class, or to turn thirty-two fouettés to the left side and to the right, on full pointe, or, with amusing results, to attempt the hummingbird beats of an entrechat huit (a vertical rocketing with eight fluttery crossings and recrossings of pointed feet on the way up) were worth an empathetic teacher's momentary commendation but not anyone's second look in the mirror, not even mine: I was wide-open to how wonderful it felt to work toward the mastery of ballet as a language and the joy of moving according to its grammar and syntax, yet I was blind to ballet itself as an art. I studied the mirror to make corrections, but it never occurred to me to look at myself in an aesthetic way. At that point, I didn't care what impression I made socially in the course of grappling with classical dance: I only cared about how vivifying it felt to address Chopin and Tchaikovsky, played by an ancient pianist on a broken-down instrument in the corner, in what I was sure was the most beautiful language ever invented. Dance mattered to me because it gave me the chance to articulate the relationship between what I felt and what I heard with my entire being, on time yet in my own momentary phrasing, with my own unstoppered "voice." And there was the collateral delight that in learning the French names of the steps I became practiced in recognizing the "speech" and, eventually, in analyzing the eloquence of the great companies that toured to my hometown. I remember sitting in the Philadelphia Academy of Music and seeing the pointed toe of a Soviet ballerina's turned-out "working leg" float up her standing leg to hover at the standing leg's knee, thereby forming a triangle, before passing to the back of the joint. This action was what I knew to call a passé, one of the very actions I was practicing in class. That epiphany alone opened my eyes to analogies in literature and film and much more, things that had nothing to do with dancing. When I say that ballet was everything then, I am being both metaphorical and almost literal, too.

We get so many different kinds of education when we're young. One lesson for me took place on the morning my eleventh-grade English teacher decided to go around the class and require each student to say aloud what she intended to do with her life. "I'm going to be a dancer," I said. The teacher, herself a large-boned woman with the strongly delineated features of a Victorian bisque doll, asked me to repeat my answer. Then she walked over to my desk, picked up my left arm by the wrist, and, to my and my classmates' surprise, brought down my bent elbow onto the desktop with a painful bang. She told me that was the wrong answer. "You are not going to be a dancer!" she said, so that everyone else could hear. "You are going to college!" She was mistaken, I said. She told me that I'd better rethink my priorities. "No," I said. It was a triumph to see her apple cheeks flush with rage. But she saw further than I did. Shortly after this class, I was wised up at a professional audition: I had the wrong bone structure, the wrong musculature, and the wrong body-mass index for the art. It was explained that, as I was already sixteen, I'd never change my physique sufficiently to make the lines that would provide the mysterious, abstract geometry of pure design under the flesh. The next afternoon, I looked at myself in the studio mirror for the first time with cold, hard recognition. I went to college.

That incident in my English class was the earliest wake-up call I registered to the reality of how ballet was regarded on the deepest level by much of the America I happened to know in the early 1960s, the very period that the Ford Foundation came to the rescue with funding of the Balanchine-Kirstein enterprise and that the great Soviet companies, as well as the Royal Ballet, were regularly touring the United States. Regardless of the entranced audiences and the prominent donors and, soon, the public funds from the newly established National Endowment for the Arts, the case for why dancing—especially the elite practice of classical ballet—ought to be supported and why young persons, in particular, should be readily exposed to it in the studio and on stage, had to be made over and over again, and it still does. Sometimes, the case for dance even has to be made because the nature of the complaint is that dance *writing* is too focused, too much about the act of dancing itself rather than about the social setting, what the dancers might be feeling, or other contextual aspects. I understand the need for extra-dance relief: it's a challenge to write about dancing, and sometimes the writer needs to help the reader take in and remember a little bit of technical information by spending three times as much space on something more everyday—the weather, a nearby bar fight, the movements of the maestro's hair when conducting the William Tell Overture—and then, in a sentence or just a phrase, slip in a fragment about an actual dance movement.

Even literary lions can be taken to task for caring too much about the subject. Several years ago, I edited an anthology of writings on American dance that included not just an essay on chorus girls but one on chorines in the Follies, by Edmund Wilson; not just articles on rhythm tap but articles on tap dancing and popular dance style by Sally Sommer, Whitney Balliett, Lincoln Kirstein, and, oh yes!, Charles Dickens; not just memoirs of dancing in after-hours clubs but poems to the club dancers by Langston Hughes; not just an invocation of dancing as a Hoodoo purification ritual but dancing as a purification ritual invoked on the page by Zora Neale Hurston. The book was thoroughly trashed on a website in a review that read, "Here, almost everything is about Dance As Art. . . . Even Michael Jackson gets 'appreciated' by a dance critic. Succeeds magnificently in making dance seem like a dead art form in a vitrine."

Was the reviewer saying that the writing wasn't good enough because the writers were too polished, too . . . artful? Or is the reviewer's message that stage dancing is in such good shape that appreciation of it is irrelevant, yet we need to learn about what vernacular dance used to be because dancing as a social practice and pleasure among the general population has become quite reduced in several ways—space, timings, choreographic patterns, team effort, standard of precision. If that is the underlying point, then I'm inclined to agree. Although financial support is increasing for dancers of color to study hip-hop and for women of all identities who wish to pursue choreography, I have yet to see much encouragement on stage or off for folk dancing where the dancers hold hands, much less for amateur social dancing by couples or for its competition form known as ballroom dancing. (The reality TV shows *Dancing with the Stars* and *So You Think You Can Dance* inspire the viewer to become an armchair judge, not a practitioner.) If you want to learn to dance with another person off stage, you have to maintain your obsession personally and, these days, privately. It's a lot of bother.

So why try? This issue long predates the anxieties over the pandemic. We live in a haphephobic age, inimical to touch. Why spend time to court frustration in learning unfamiliar steps and body positions while embracing a partner—in a situation that requires space to maneuver and where you might be mocked by onlookers, or, during the pandemic, infected by them—when you can learn a solo routine in place through TikTok (some are ingenious, too) and can choose whether or not to display your dance-educated self online. Of course, TikTokkers can work as simultaneous soloists in pairs or even groups; theoretically, they could take a ballroom-standard closed frame (embrace) with one another and try an English quickstep up the kitchen wall—something not too far distant from one of the charming special effects that the director Steven Spielberg and choreographer Justin Peck conspired to pull off in their Hollywood redoing of *West Side Story*. Still, the beauty of TikTok is that you don't have to touch anyone else if you're fine with dancing with yourself, regardless of whether you decide to become a private dancer for millions of followers as well. And although the TikTok challenges do ask that you learn a little dance, the idea of doing that by yourself reinforces the idea of dancing alone in general. This cultural preference for soloism goes beyond TikTok: it affects the stage. In this century, I've seen many "modern" and "postmodern" programs where entire regiments of dancers perform what are, essentially, simultaneous solos. Some of these works are masterpieces, meditations on the essential solitude of the human condition: Vaslav Nijinsky's *L'Après-midi d'un Faune* or the second movement of Paul Taylor's *Esplanade*—works where figures are engaged in much expressive interaction yet never touch. Some entire dance practices are conveyed by soloists, for instance rhythm tap or Japanese Noh. However, the great examples are exceptions.

When did this soloism overtake us? The country had once danced and watched dancing for pleasure, invented animal dances in juke joints, cheered the silk-stepping Castles, practiced aerials in the Lindy, Big Appled to the big bands, conjugated its Latin at the Palladium, and crowded into theaters and opera houses and gymnasia to sashay around shahs and sylphides during World War II's ballet boom. In the mid-1950s, my second-grade teacher, a student at Arthur Murray's in her spare time, would get the entire class on our feet in the aisles as a kind of seventh-inning stretch during geography or social studies to learn the cha-cha-cha. Xavier Cugat at school, Tin Pan Alley and doo-wop on the radio at home, 45 rpm records of Rodgers and Hammerstein musicals to fall asleep by—Heaven!

And now, Purgatory. At the beginning of my senior year, I made the obligatory trip to look at colleges. My friends at the Philadelphia High School for Girls were true whiz kids (this one taught herself Russian, that one was taking her math classes at the University of Pennsylvania, another one was concertizing now and then as a classical pianist, and so on). I didn't breathe that Olympian air; however, my father and his family did. They nearly all went to Harvard or the sister school, Radcliffe, on scholarship as part of the Jewish quota, traveling to classes on the streetcar from home, and there was an expectation that I'd follow, though surely by now in a campus dorm. Girls weren't welcome to matriculate as undergrads at Harvard in the 1960s, but a large group from my class applied to Radcliffe; I threw my hat in the ring, too. Alas, during my interview at Radcliffe, the admissions officer who met with me was not pleased to learn that I'd taken ten ballet classes a week during three years of high school. She remarked that, of course, as a Radcliffe student I'd give up all thoughts of dance and buckle down to my important studies. That was a triggering moment. Remembering my bullying English teacher, I wasn't going to let this philistine get away with anything, either. By then, I'd given up all of my ballet classes, yet my connection to dancing was deeper than I realized: I attended performances as often as I could, and I read about the history of ballet obsessively. So I revved up my rhetoric at the interview and launched into an impassioned explanation of how much ballet dancing meant to me, that I'd never abandon it, and, yada yada yada, QED. When I walked out of the office, my velvet fedora askew and sweat pouring down my cheeks, I walked out of any hope of attending Radcliffe.

Truth has consequences. Once again, my obsession with dancing proved not to be to my advantage; however, I'd learned another important lesson: for whatever reason and by means I shall never understand, dancing had claimed me. To this day, I have no idea why me, but I do know that I am one of countless individuals who have been singled out by the Fates for a vassal's service to dance in general and ballet in particular.

America's legacy of disapproving attitudes toward dancing goes back at least as far as seventeenth-century Protestant immigrants who sailed here from persecution in Europe. The dance historian Ann Wagner has chronicled them expansively and authoritatively in *Adversaries of Dance: From the Puritans to the Present* (1997), her book about the long history of efforts to explain or persuade why dance should *not* matter in this country, a book that has yet to be rivaled in scope or focus with respect to this subject. Wagner contends that the deeply rooted opposition to dancing among certain Protestant denominations and fundamentalist groups originated in white men who sought to control the display of sexuality by women. True in many cases, yet my childhood experiences also suggest that the situation is more complex—that women have proved themselves adversaries to dance as well.

I'm still stunned, all these years later, by a moment between an adult and a small child that I chanced upon in the lobby of the New York State Theater during the 1990s, following an exultant performance by New York City Ballet and students from the School of American Ballet of George Balanchine's production of *The Nutcracker.* In the midst of hundreds of families, energized and happy, milling around by the box office windows, not wanting to leave quite yet, was a slim, tall, fair-haired beauty, perhaps in her late thirties, exquisitely coiffed and wearing a full-length fur. Alas, she was extremely irritable: a little girl (perhaps eight or nine years old) in front of her wasn't moving fast enough in buttoning up her Chesterfield coat with the velvet collar. The woman, whom I took to be the girl's mother, discovered that speaking sharply to the child wasn't effective in moving her along. And so she went to Plan B: pulling back one arm, she delivered a haymaker to the girl's cheek. The child burst into tears. This was following a ballet that, for two hours, had purveyed imagery of moderation when kids are being mischievous and of beauty and high spirits when they've demonstrated noble initiative. I'm referring to the imagery of the work as it is given to the paying audience, of course. In her memoir, *Swan Dive* (2021), NYCB soloist Georgina Pazcoguin makes it clear that not everyone in the company who performs this *Nutcracker* today thinks of it as anything more treasured than an old war horse.

Speaking of slaps at NYCB, there is quite a prominent one in Peter Martins's *Romeo + Juliet* of 2007, where Lord Capulet slaps his daughter, something he only intimates he'll do in Shakespeare's play. Or there was. A couple of years ago, the company management removed it. Still, out of respect for reality, I think the slap should have been left in the action. In fact, the offensive hand could shift at alternate performances from the Lord to the Lady. *West Side Story*, another *Romeo and Juliet* retelling, cleverly sidesteps the entire issue of parenting as the imposition of authorized power by removing parents altogether, leaving only a few, mostly disdained, parental subs. (This may help to account for some of the show's appeal as a daydream writ large to aspiring middle-school, high school, and overnight-camp thespians.)

Of all the Balanchine ballets for that memorable lobby event to have followed, *The Nutcracker* provides the harshest irony. If you've seen Balanchine's production, you know that the several tender mother-child relationships in it are central to the ballet's emotion and, ultimately, to its meaning. There are Mrs. Stahlbaum and her own children, Marie and Fritz, in act 1; and, in act 2, there are the Sugar Plum Fairy and the flock of little girl angels she oversees. Later, in a comic reversal, there is a towering Mother Ginger clown and her Polichinelle children, who live under her circus tent of a skirt. And there is the mystical relationship of the ultimate feminine figure in the work—the Christmas tree that grows to scrape the sky, becoming, in Balanchine's term, "the ballerina" of this imaginative world. A vision of snowflakes embodied as female dancers whirl through the forest in geometric configurations, waltzing representations of pure Nature—beautiful and impersonal, like the Alps of Switzerland, which inspired Hans Christian Andersen's novella *The Ice-Maiden* (1861), another winter story Balanchine returned to throughout his career. However, the snowflakes are distinct from *The Nutcracker*'s various maternal figures, who are always presented as individuals in the ballet's realistic first act and who, in the second act, offer ideals or at least models to follow to hospitality, mystery, and entertainment. The Sugar Plum Fairy's ultimate gift to Marie and the now-transformed Nutcracker Prince is to send them, filled with images of grace and fun, into the night sky on a reindeer sleigh. Perhaps the weeping child I saw in the lobby was able to retain for herself a memory of that flight into the wonder world where beauty and kindness and patience reliably matter.

Childhood in the theater is a construct, a creation. Just because children are cast as characters who are supposed to *be* children does not ensure that the performers persuasively convey the idea of young human beings—with their complex, dynamic selves continually recalibrating from moment to moment, now animalistic, now scientifically curious, now secretive or thoughtless, now angelically open-hearted. Nor is a child necessarily intended to signify a child in the chronological sense. The cupids of Renaissance painting have the bodies of toddlers or preschoolers but often the expressions of grown satyrs from ancient art. There is the material body and the immaterial spirit or interior life. We often presume that they are in sync, but some artists want us to consider situations where they aren't.

An example is the only child in Doris Humphrey's dance *Day on Earth* (1947), a succinct allegory of human life as love, work, sorrow, and regeneration, set to Aaron Copland's Piano Sonata, described by the composer as "absolute music." Yet not entirely absolute: as John Mueller, the scholar of dance films, meticulously explained in "Masterpieces by Doris Humphrey and Aaron Copland," in the February 1979 issue of *Dance Magazine,* the score is built on three main motifs, as are the three sections of Humphrey's choreography. The third section, which begins with the child's death and concludes with her as the only figure "alive," is where the work's explicit magic resides in the music as well. *Day on Earth* requires four dancers: an Everyman; a maiden whom he fancies and who disappears when he kisses her; a mother who gives birth symbolically to a little girl (portrayed by a child of ten or eleven) and who then symbolically buries her prematurely "dead" child before dying herself; and the child, who at first skips and plays, then stretches out unmoving. The man goes back to work alone, though with increasing weakness, and finally he stretches out, too. The maiden returns and, with the other adults, lies down. Once the three adults are disempowered, the child rises up, and alone, chin in hand, she considers existence. This child is not another reader of *The Five Little Peppers and How They Grew* or even of Eleanor Estes's *The Hundred Dresses.* This is an elementary-school reader of Jean-Paul Sartre's *Existentialism.*

Balanchine's choreography for children, a mixture of what

they do well and what challenges them to do well, leaves the impression of them as individuals engaging in this common activity because they want to. This obtains even when they're all dancing the same steps to the same musical counts and are identically costumed: perhaps he well remembered how some of the children's roles he danced as a student at the Mariinsky Ballet felt to perform, although my guess is that, given his temperament and experience, he was far more concerned with directing our attention where he wanted it to go for reasons having to do with the work at hand rather than life remembrances. Sometimes, our focus is meant to be on the ensemble of children in a dance; and sometimes it is meant to be on the adult soloist (usually a danseuse) for whom the children serve as a context, as a distraction, as a frame, or even as packaging. Sometimes, as with the little Polichinelles who spring from under Mother Ginger's gigantic skirt (the witticism of the construction is that it is also a theater), they shoot their steps through space with a quicksilver joy; and sometimes their dancing is only a glorified running walk, but on the children, aiming to do the steps just right, the simple action offers the kind of breath-holding suspense that even an adult can feel when having to carry a goblet filled a little too high and only the surface tension of the liquid keeps the wine from spilling over the rim.

In *Nutcracker*'s dance of the Angels in act 2, two lines of the tiny girls in their instep-length dresses, reminiscent of women's gowns from Slavic Georgia, have the choreographic mission to travel at a specific tempo, equally spaced along two arms of a full-stage, religiously evocative X without crashing in the middle. The

Angels have the responsibility of professional dancers to meet their challenge, and their coaches help them to understand how to meet those responsibilities as troupers. But no one would mistake any of them for Thomas Hardy's prematurely aged Old Father Time; the Angels are little girls fulfilling an important requirement whose demands are commensurate with their age and experience as dancers. Their commitment to the challenge is part of the choreography, and the purpose of building it in is so the smallest dancers can exemplify the high seriousness of purpose that Balanchine ascribed to dancing, with the result that the children appear at their loveliest to a big audience, in a big theater, at every performance.

The tiniest details of production matter as meaning. Even their golden Karinska headpieces are puns on both a halo and the wide brim of a child's boater.

And yet these child Angels don't look drilled; they look awed—an important aspect to some of Balanchine's works for adult dancers, too. (That breath-holding suspense of the Angels' dance is also embedded in the courtly opening walks that unite the principal couple of "Diamonds" in *Jewels,* when they approach one another from distant points of the stage, as if they had traversed the earth from opposite directions to get there.) The youngsters convey the sense that they are thrilled to be in this moment in this space, where the party is for them yet not about them—where the subject of their participation is something larger. A similar effect is provided by the tiny couples of his "Tempo di Valse: Garland Dance from 'The Sleeping Beauty'"; by the girls who serve as the measurements of the day in "Dance of the Golden Hours" in act 3 of *Coppélia;* by the skittering forest creatures of *A Midsummer Night's Dream;* by the dances that render the children who perform them with touching exactness to be commedia dell'arte miniatures of adult dancers in *Harlequinade;* and by the quartet of solemn attendants to the ballerina in the 1981 version of *Mozartiana.* One roots for the faceted childhood that Balanchine confected for them, where they joyously behave and nobly serve. He did not make parts for the kids to express their personal emotions, ambitions, or deep thoughts. And yet, paradoxically, in pouring out energy to make the steps and gestures real and fine, the children convey an ineffable sense of interior life.

Children are also asked to serve, without projecting self-consciousness, as elements in the animated stage architecture that Balanchine built from comparative placements of limbs and faces, feet and shins, forearms and hands, child and adult.

Did Balanchine's early fascination in Petrograd with the avant-garde and circuslike experiments of choreographers and theater directors, often grouped together under the term constructivism, lead to some of the architectural groupings and intricate ensemble arrangements that can be found throughout his mid- and late career work as well as in the dances he made in the 1920s and 1930s? It's true that Serge Diaghilev, having hired Balanchine as his last choreographer, to succeed the brilliantly unpredictable neoclassicist Bronislava Nijinska, took the young prodigy (somewhat reluctantly, it seems) through the great art museums of continental Europe for an education in aesthetics; one can see what he learned right in his choreography. However, while still in the

USSR, Balanchine absorbed artistic lessons from the greatest of Russian painters, beginning with the medieval masters of the icons; and among the feverish experiments in dance and live theater of his moment, he was taken by the productions of Kasyan Goleizovsky (1892–1970), who incorporated acrobatics into his efforts for his Moscow Chamber Ballet. In 1923, shortly before leaving the Soviet Union permanently, Balanchine worked directly with the group known as FEKS (The Fabricators of Eccentricities, Inc.). As his contemporary Yuri Slonimsky observed, the actor and stage director Vsevolod Meyerhold (1874–1940)—whose theatrical innovations included his attempts to return acting to its roots in commedia dell'arte and whose techniques linking the actor's psychology and learned gestures led his dying frenemy Konstantin Stanislavski to declare Meyerhold his only remaining heir in the theater—"was the teacher of everyone—including Balanchine."

Balanchine himself performed in Fyodor Lopukhov's narrative spectacle *Tanzsynfonia* or, in English, *Dance Symphony: The Magnificence of the Universe* (1923), to the Fourth Symphony of Beethoven, a ballet (in today's parlance) "canceled" by the Soviet authorities after one performance for its (in yesterday's parlance) "bourgeois formalism." Lopukhov's four-movement ballet certainly had a scenario, which was nothing less than the beginnings of life on earth and its evolution to produce a human society capable of high art: Lincoln Kirstein describes it in his entry for *Tanzsynfonia* in *Movement and Metaphor* (1971), a description of fifty canonic theatrical dances in the West from 1573 to 1968. Some thirty-five years ago, some of the ballet was reconstructed by Lopukhov's son and Nikita Dolgushin, a dancer and teacher with knowledge of the period, and—when ballet is amazing, it really is amazing—the entire *Tanzsynfonia* was reconstructed to the best of its ability by a ballet academy in Japan (a country with some of the most devoted classical dancers and classical dance audiences in the world). I've seen films of each reconstruction, and what I can say is that the adagio, for two ballerinas in white tutus and on pointe (originally Alexandra Danilova and Lidia Ivanova), and a male corps de ballet in black, has an impersonal— even scientific—tone of a process steadily evolving. The twin ballerinas form a goddess dyad, acknowledging no one; they are lifted overhead by the corps so that they seem to sail, icebergs on dark waters. The eyes of the audience are indeed directed all over the stage by the stately choreography, including upward. One also thinks of Balanchine's Siren, in his *Prodigal Son,* being hoisted to the shoulders of the corps of goons, and, in a very different context, the Germanic score (Paul Hindemith this time) and dramatis personae of two ballerinas and a male corps in his *Kammermusik No. 2.*

While still in the USSR, Balanchine worked in theaters of all genres and sizes, choreographing for plays and cabarets, playing piano for silent films, devising dances for unconventional auditoria. Thanks to Arlene Croce, whose *Ballet Review* published the English translation of Slonimsky's memoir, to the scholarly critic Robert Greskovic, and to the many other scholars and writers intoxicated by the genius of Russian/Soviet dancing in those few early anything-goes years of the 1920s—including the late Nancy Van Norman Baer and the late Sally Banes, the Ballets

Russes and Bronislava Nijinska specialist Lynn Garafola, and the three Elizabeths of Soviet dance history: Elizabeth Souritz, Elizabeth Kendall, and Elizabeth Kattner—English-speaking readers have gotten a remarkably detailed picture of the newborn Soviet dance world more than a century after it was snuffed out. (That scene consists of actual reconstructions of machine dances and farces for uniformed factory workers and at least one mystifying venture—the cubo-futurist opera *Victory over the Sun,* of 1913—where world myth morphs into the poetry of sci-fi and which, over the past century, has enjoyed more attempts to reconstruct it than the two original performances that gave it life.) Balanchine's darkest ballets are no longer performed; however, the impersonality of *Tanzsynfonia* and the experiments with breaking through the fourth wall of the proscenium arch can still be glimpsed in his repertory. He constructed ensembles of varying levels, building his dances upward as well as wide and deep. He made corps groupings into living decor. He used the wings as permeable borders. Children participate in these designs. When, in the Christmas Eve party in act 1 of *The Nutcracker,* the audience sees the adult version and the children's version of a formal courting dance for couples, it is like finding a finished building and the maquette alongside—and the maquette is the more delightful.

A choreographer who learned another Balanchine lesson—about relating dancers of different heights and physiques in stereotypical relationships with a twist, to dramatic as well as innovative effect—is Paul Taylor. The tragicomedy of his *Three Epitaphs* is based on the dancers' descending heights. The wrenching disintegration of the American family that is the subject of *Big Bertha* requires that the daughter be smaller than the mother in order for their roles to be immediately understood. The last moments of his *Esplanade*—when one of the women steps downstage center directly to the audience and opens her arms to embrace us all ("This dance is you, Audience")—is particularly poignant when that dancer is small in stature: her childlike impression delivers a monumental gift to those who watch her. It's as if the most important statement one could make can be articulated only in gesture, like the "dumb show" in *Hamlet*. When Taylor choreographed *Esplanade,* in the early 1970s, he had just been forced by injury to give up dancing. Choreography had become the sole door open to him in dance, and *Esplanade* was the first of his postdancer dances in which he walked through it, renewed.

That valedictory moment of *Esplanade*—where the last dancer left on stage breaks the fourth wall in order to create what the theologian Martin Buber called an I-Thou connection with the audience—for me invokes Isadora Duncan, who was famously associated with I-Thou relationships between herself and the audience. Of course, she did not see that will as a force generated by herself only. Duncan once claimed that even when she was the lone dancer on stage, she "never danced a solo," a somewhat enigmatic statement, although, as a reader of Walt Whitman's poetry, she may have been thinking of his declaration that he, one sensibility alone, nevertheless "contain[ed] multitudes." Isadora's embrace reaching through the fourth wall was an open interpretation of Whitman. Nearly a century later, audiences learned that the poet was close to Taylor's heart as well, as his late masterpiece *Beloved Renegade* exemplifies.

For practical reasons (and sometimes, as with the character of the raped and ravaged daughter in Taylor's *Big Bertha,* moral ones) adults are asked to impersonate small children in theatrical dances. However, to isolate ways in which choreographers create childhood, it's more useful to compare dances made for—and still performed by—child dancers of about the same age and level of training. An illustrative pairing is Balanchine's "Waltz of the Golden Hours," for twenty-four adolescent girls and a female soloist, in the third act of NYCB's *Coppélia,* and the Children's Polonaise and Mazurka for twelve boy-girl couples of the same age (about eleven to thirteen), choreographed by Marius Petipa as one of his revisions to the third-act wedding celebration of *Paquita.* For both dances, the children performing are already veterans of at least a couple of years of classes in the fundamentals of classical technique but, in most cases, not yet past their growth spurts. My memories of having seen both dances in the theater were the guides to my thought; in addition, as aide-mémoire for steps and patterns, I used films on YouTube. Especially helpful was a portion of the "Waltz of the Golden Hours" in a PBS telecast of NYCB's *Coppélia* in 1978, featuring company member Sheryl Ware as the adult soloist, dancing among the children with nuance, exactitude, musicality, and almost microscopic detail. At YouTube, I also found helpful a brief, on-camera interview with one of the child Hours from another company's *Coppélia,* the Pacific Northwest Ballet production (which also uses the Alexandra Danilova–Balanchine choreography).

Little in dance history is simple; fact-checking of topics before the twentieth century is frequently provisional. So, as one possible way to consider the innovation of Balanchine's choreography (not knowing exactly what other models he might have had in mind), I sought out a Russian film of the late Sergei Vikharev's very different staging of the same music in his *Coppélia* of 2009 for the Bolshoi Ballet, a reconstruction from period notation now at the Harvard Theatre Collection.

The production history of the ballet's Russian stagings is rather intricate. Although the original *Coppélia* in 1870 was produced in Paris with choreography by Arthur Saint-Léon, the Marius Petipa Society's website explains that the ballet's several productions in Russia involved, all in all, a handful of choreographers, beginning with, yet not exclusively, Petipa. In 1904, however, Petipa revived the production to which those several ballet masters had contributed; it was his last version, and that is the *Coppélia* that has served as the model of most subsequent productions, including, more or less, that of Balanchine and Danilova at NYCB. Vikharev's reconstructed version of the Hours waltz (with "Golden" omitted from the title and whose choreographer theoretically could have been Petipa and/or Lev Ivanov and/or Joseph Hansen and/or Enrico Cecchetti or perhaps, in some aspect, Saint-Léon) gives us an ensemble of twenty-four adult danseuses with no soloist.

The high point of this version is when the dancers arrange themselves in a large circle and each woman takes one pirouette in place seriatim—an image of the hours, one by one, whirling by within their larger orbit of the firmament. (The costumes of

Vikharev's reconstruction indicate that each group of six dancers is meant to be affiliated with a specific quarter of the day, with the six dancers for the nighttime hours in dresses and mantillas that look black or midnight blue.) The patterns tend to be serried ranks. On the other hand, Balanchine's transposition of the waltz to little girls constantly moving in groups of three and rising and falling into poses of several levels addresses an audience that, by the mid-1970s, when this ballet was brought into NYCB's repertoire, was accustomed from television, film, and early videos to much faster visual change than were the audiences of 1904.

His child dancers wear soft shoes; however, their insteps are strongly stretched in half-point turns, and they perform many of the same steps and leaps as Vikharev's reconstruction assigns the adult corps de ballet, the major difference being that Balanchine's children occupy the stage entirely for only half the number, with the adult soloist magnetizing the audience for the other half. Both Balanchine's children and Vikharev's adults only turn single revolutions when they pirouette in place. These are not prima *ballerine*—not Pierina Legnani or Mathilde Kchessinskaya, who mastered the spectacular thirty-two fouettés seriatim. Still, by 1904, a single pirouette in place would be a maneuver that an entire adult corps could reliably deliver on pointe. Seven decades later, Balanchine translated the adults' technique to little children (who had, of course, been carefully schooled by teachers he had hired).

Classical dancing—not only classical ballet but the court dances of Cambodia, Thailand, Indonesia, Korea, Okinawa, and Japan, as well as the major dance traditions of India (Bharata Natyam, Odissi, Kachipudi, and so on)—is built on such details. This is also the case for the long-standing community dance traditions of Native Americans and Canadian First Peoples, the ancient hulas of Hawai'i, and the ceremonial dances of Western Africa. They are exclusive, treasured, and considered standards of beauty and spirituality by virtue of the fact that it takes an entire childhood and adolescence of constant practice to begin to learn them and then the better part of a lifetime to understand why it matters that they are being preserved—matters to both one's culture or tribe and to oneself personally. Many of the details are heirlooms from the past, and adherence to them in dance—where the materials are the perishable human body, ineffable ideas concerning what the body should do when, and invisible bridges of correspondence to music—provides a hope for the sustained life of humanity beyond the inevitable death of every practitioner. Without adherence to the past, innovation not only wouldn't be valued but wouldn't be recognizable as innovation.

For the Children's Polonaise and Mazurka, I used a film from 2012 of dancers from Saint Petersburg's Vaganova Academy in the current Mariinsky production of *Paquita,* which, in 2019, I saw live several times during the Mariinsky's visit to the Kennedy Center. I also checked it against a recent film of children from the Bolshoi's school in the Moscow company's current *Paquita.* And thanks to the generosity of PNB's education manager Doug Fullington, I had access to a film of the version of the Children's dances that he personally staged for ballet students of the Bayerisches Staatsballett, in Munich, as a member of the team of dance historian–stagers, headed by Alexei Ratmansky, who reconstructed Petipa's 1881 revival of the full *Paquita*. The Children's Polonaise and Mazurka, one dance in two parts, belongs to that new production. To stage it, Fullington—who, like Ratmansky, reads the Stepanov notation system, in which a great swath of Petipa's choreography was recorded by his assistant Nikolai Sergueeff—worked from the notations of the dance at the Harvard Theatre Collection, where the Sergueeff notations now reside.

I was fascinated by some discrepancies between the version for the Munich children and those for the students of the Mariinsky and the Bolshoi. The Polonaise, for instance, though brief, has a tiny additional accent in the walk of Fullington's staging, there are some differences midway through between what he asked the German children to do and what is done in Russia, and his ending for the children is very different: in the version that Fullington staged, based on the notations, the tuneful music sweeps the couples off into the wings; they are a kind of vision. In the Russian companies' versions, the child couples are brought forward nearly to the edge of the stage to face the audience and, on the last notes of the music, to bow and accept applause.

My quest for information brought other new information. I didn't realize, for example, that the Children's Polonaise and Mazurka from Petipa's *Paquita* of 1881 is not rare. Students at the Metropolitan Ballet school in the Jenkintown neighborhood of Philadelphia, for example, have the dance in the repertory of classical works that the school's performing arm dances. How many other children's groups perform this ballet in the United States? Another surprise (contained in the online catalogue raisonné for

Balanchine on the website of the George Balanchine Foundation, www.balanchine.org) offers the likelihood, attested to by one of Balanchine's Imperial Ballet School classmates, that, in 1917, when Balanchine was around thirteen years old and a student at the Mariinsky school, he performed in this dance himself.

"You have to be super-prepared, physically and mentally," one of the girls in the Golden Hours waltz explains in the film for the Pacific Northwest Ballet production of *Coppélia,* staged (and partially choreographed anew) by Balanchine and Alexandra Danilova. Those are the words of a professional indeed. And yet, the effect of the dance—its accomplished little girls waltzing and running and pacing while holding hands and kneeling to become a living surround for the soloist's leaps and spins and her subtle reorientations of the body—is of pure pleasure, a liquefaction of continuous movement, enacted by beings who do not appear to break a sweat. The children are always in motion, yet they are never exposed beyond their ability to carry off this illusion of perpetual delight. It was only in comparing this dance to the Children's dance in *Paquita* that I perceived the magic distractions that Balanchine had slipped throughout the Dance of the Hours. He continuously divides and subdivides the twelve figures into groups and subgroups. He alternates levels—jumps, half-toe, kneeling, the children's gestures and turns of the head answering the soloist's airborne sorties, as if they were the wind beneath her sails. The children and the soloist are bound up together: *their* dance matters because *her* dance matters, and vice versa. We are inside both the clock time to which all the dancers on stage must pay obeisance and the more profound intuition of passing time in each dancer, which arises from each person's sense of where she is in space as measured against where other dancers are and where her dancing is in the choreographic phrase. (In ensemble dances, misalignments can eventuate in disaster—the premise of the comedy of the "Mistake Waltz" in Jerome Robbins's ballet comedy *The Concert*.)

Balanchine's ballets, even the ones with stories, are, happily, without obvious moral; their pleasures are guided by the music, the choreographic plan, often the costumes and sometimes the sets, and, above all, the dancing. Nevertheless, for those who care to think about them, they do yield implications. Take Balanchine's "Waltz of the Golden Hours" in the Balanchine-Danilova *Coppélia:* twelve little girls engaged in the serious study of ballet, pretty in pink, skim around the stage as the Hours; at their center is a grown-up ballerina, providing not only a focus for the audience and a role to showcase a valued soloist but also a brilliant example of the dancing skills the students are studying to master. Balanchine offers this kind of contrast in age and proportions elsewhere in his repertoire. The reasons for providing it are certainly practical, yet the continual, dreamlike comparison both intensifies our interest in the adult and frees the children from having to be perfect—that is, perfectly matched in silhouette and muscular tension, as well as in the steps and gestures. The deep beauty, to me, of this dance and its casting is that the children look spirited, free, and individual, while pursuing a common goal, and that the soloist—once a young ballet student herself—

magnifies those qualities through craft and personal ability. The dance seems apt for a society whose political center is—or, by this writing, perhaps once was—the U.S. Constitution.

However, Petipa's nineteenth-century polonaise and mazurka for children, though similar to the "Hours" in a few ways (its twelve boy-girl couples are mostly pre-adolescent and with several years of ballet technique behind them, and their choreography is mostly allegro in speed and spirit), is also more severe, exposing of any error, and so, one might say, in terms of anxiety level, it is the more challenging, the harder of the two in terms of the stress it places on the dancers. The key challenge of the Petipa dance is in the choreographic units into which the children are assigned. On what might be called the micro level, they are nearly always part of a dyad; sometimes, the partners perform the same steps in the same way, and sometimes they are divided by different, gender-specific steps. The step patterns for the group—circles, lines, partner-changing weaves—derived from folk dance, are tightly spaced and tightly timed. That is an aspect of the choreography's virtuosity, whether, as here, enunciated by children or in adult folk-dance companies. In the middle of the dance, the music softens and slows and the girls become part of a circle in the center while the boys (costumed as Napoleonic hussars) become part of a larger, protective circle around them. The action thereby affirms an ancient societal order that is patriarchal, which is, perhaps, why the choreographer Bronislava Nijinska, creator of the Ballets Russes masterpiece *Les Noces,* was not a fan of this dance. At the end, all twenty-four dancers join hands grapevine fashion—boy-girl, boy-girl—and, in one swaying line, everybody, synchronized to every other body, each dancer identically changing the body's weight via steps magnetized to the earth, advances as one being toward the audience—a definitive statement of tribal identity.

The first time I saw the Children's Polonaise and Mazurka live, it was performed in the mid-1980s by students from the Leningrad State Choreographic Institute, as the Vaganova Academy was then named. The exacting principles it embodied seemed at once shocking and sacred. In the much more recent performances by the Mariinsky company in Washington, D.C., where the children were provided again by the company's attendant school in Saint Petersburg, the audience also greeted the work with an intake of breath at the start before loudly punctuating the performance with displays of pleasure. In part, I thought, the reception must be occasioned by the startling yet enjoyable synchrony, which triggers our innate enjoyment of seeing living beings subsumed into symmetrical patterning, presenting the possibility that fallible creatures can, at least momentarily, achieve superhuman perfection. Choreographers exploit this inevitable enjoyment in situations as various as the four little swans in *Swan Lake* and the kick lines of the Rockettes. But the fact that small children are producing this synchrony without any help beyond their training and rehearsal brings adults and other children, too, to amazement. There is something in it of the miraculous, but also, for this or that audience member, something potentially unpleasant. One may ask what had to be done to achieve this unnatural result from children? Something more damaging than the imposition of discipline that education imposes on every child? But suppose the child *wants* to achieve the effect? Again, here are the words of the little PNB Golden Hours dancer, spoken in pride: "We have to be super-prepared physically and mentally." And they were uttered in speaking of the Balanchine dance that appears to let children use their training to exult in the golden hours of their childhood.

Where did Petipa get the idea for making his children's dance? Children have nothing to do with the story of *Paquita,* and neither the dances nor Petipa's music for them by Ludwig Minkus have anything to do with the ballet's location in Spain. Most immediately, one imagines, this children's interlude provided a chance for the Imperial Ballet School to display the excellence of its training and its students as well as a breather for the rest of the cast and, perhaps, some time to change scenery backstage. Its dislocation from its theatrical context was no more problematic for most of the audience than the fact that the ballerinas of the Imperial Ballet would wear their own jewels in whatever role they happened to perform, regardless of who or where they were supposed to be. However, all that said, some balletgoers continue to wonder why the Children's Polonaise and Mazurka was inserted into *Paquita*.

Here are my ruminations.

In every production of the dance I've seen, there is a common feature to the children's costumes. The boys always wear scarlet vests or off-the-shoulder capes and sometimes have red stripes on their trousers or red boots. And in all but the Ratmansky reconstruction of *Paquita* in Munich (where the girls are dressed entirely in white), girls wear costumes that are largely white yet edged or decorated with red features. (In the case of the Mariinsky production, they also wear beautiful red, soft-soled shoes.) Red costumes were a memorable part of this ballet from the beginning. The original *Paquita* was given its premiere in 1846 by the Paris Opéra Ballet, in choreography by Joseph Mazilier to a score by Édouard Deldevez (both men now practically forgotten), as a vehicle for the Romantic star Carlotta Grisi, who had made a great success there five years earlier as the first Giselle.

By 1846, though, the Parisian ballet public no longer had a taste or much tolerance for men in ballets, and many of the male figures in the corps de ballet were played by danseuses in male costumes, as travesty roles. Although the original male lead, named Lucien, opposite Grisi's Paquita, was danced by Marius Petipa's bravura brother Lucien, the historian Ivor Guest consulted period newspaper reviews and noted in his landmark study *The Romantic Ballet in Paris* (2008) that "in the first act, which was full of Spanish and Gypsy dancing, local color abounded. The dances were full of character, particularly the *pas des manteaux,* a sort of *cachucha* [a lively, even frisky Hispanic dance, often with castanets and the torso carried off the plumb line, using steps that are close to the ground] performed in the manner of the Viennese children by the *corps de ballet,* half of them dressed in male attire and brandishing voluminous red cloaks with which they enveloped themselves and their partners." So the original production of *Paquita* provided Petipa a precedent for the mazurka, for its evocation of children, for the element in it of romance, and possibly for the look of the costumes. But who were "the Viennese Children"?

During the nineteenth century and the early twentieth, companies of dancing children traveled the globe, sometimes on tour for several years in succession, and overseen by alarmingly few adults. The Viennese Children was a celebrated example. Founded in the earlier 1840s by Josephine Weiss (1805–1852), an erstwhile soloist and later a ballet mistress at several ballet companies in Austria, the troupe consisted of forty-eight ballet girls between the ages of six and approximately fourteen. Choreography, tutelage, and chaperoning were the province of the founder, and the costumes were apparently spectacular. After performing throughout Europe and in Great Britain, in 1846 the children embarked on a two-year tour of the continental United States. The year before, Théôphile Gautier had reviewed their debut at the Paris Opéra. (Gautier's reviews are found in Ivor Guest's collection *Gautier on Dance,* published in 1986.) After a long preamble in which he laced into the very idea of child prodigies forced to dance for the public, he gave the Viennese Children a rave. And he described a passage that also could have accounted for the ending of Petipa's dance for children in *Paquita:*

> There was a delightful moment when the whole troupe, forming a single line stretching from one wing to the other, advanced from the back of the stage to the footlights balancing on one leg. Not one of those microscopic feet was behind by a thousandth of a second. They alighted as if moved by a single mind.
>
> The *hongroise,* which was interpolated into the ball scene of the second act, gave no less pleasure. Half the troupe, dressed in male costume, served as partners to the others. You cannot imagine the rapidity and daring of those little Hungarians.

It seems clear to me that Petipa was calling on memories of these dancers, in Josephine Weiss's choreography, in choreographing his Children's Polonaise and Mazurka in 1881. However, no travesty boys for him! Not only was bravura dancer Lucien Petipa the first male lead of *Paquita* as well as Marius's brother, but *Paquita* was the first ballet that Marius staged in Russia, and he danced Lucien's part there. The Russian public did not have the same problems as Parisians with men in ballet. In fact, in Saint Petersburg, the esteemed, Swedish-born Christian Johansson was setting standards for male dancing on stage—where he was a premier danseur, much admired for his nobility and grace—and in the classroom, where, formally added to the faculty of the Imperial School in 1869, he collaborated with Petipa to strengthen male dancing, especially through his teaching of the French school of technique developed by Auguste Vestris and a direct line of subsequent ballet masters. The boys of the Children's Polonaise and Mazurka—with their unimpeachable manners, their musicality, their strong yet elegant partnering of their girl partners— helped Saint Petersburg replace Paris as the nerve center of the world's ballet. The boys stayed in the picture. (Josephine Weiss, though, did not. After a difficult U.S. tour, she and the Viennese Children made a second appearance in Saint Louis, where Weiss was overheard to scream at the children, causing some to weep, and bystanders to ask her to please pipe down. One day, in her late forties, she suddenly died, and that was the end of the Viennese Children.)

So, we have a contradiction concerning Weiss and her charges.

On the basis of how the children look while dancing on stage, Gautier salutes her. "The very glimpse of those pretty pink and white faces, those little chubby arms and those dimpled shoulders is enough to convince you that this troupe of cherubs has not acquired its talents at the cost of torture," he writes. "Mme Weiss seems to be as good a teacher as she is skillful as a ballet mistress." But the memoirist who overheard her screaming at the children in America suggests the possibility that she was either at her wits' end after an exhausting travel and performance schedule or that her offstage treatment of the children could be, pace Gautier, emotionally brutal. Whatever the answer, I believe that her energies and the artistry of the children from two centuries ago can still be glimpsed in the "ephemeral" art of dance.

In the forty years I actively reviewed theatrical dancing on both U.S. coasts, there were several performances when I was in a quandary about whether the stage events I watched could be considered a cry for help. Once, I had no doubts and reviewed the show for the *Village Voice* as an instance of child abuse. An infant under a year old was positioned for more than five minutes between two sound speakers of monstrous size and assaulted with ear-splitting rock music while the baby screamed to kingdom come. Then the star of the show grasped the infant under its arms and—as it continued to scream—lifted it overhead. As a pièce de résistance, he lifted up his fabric tunic or shirt, showed that he was naked under it, and flashed the baby. As it happened, the woman who had brought the child to the performance—its mother? its caregiver?—stood directly behind me with its stroller and did nothing. The readers of the *Voice* did nothing. The individuals at the theater who had contracted the show did nothing. I still regret that I merely reviewed this "avant-garde" presentation: I should have walked to the front of the performing area and screamed myself to kill the lights and stop the proceedings.

But what should one think when confronted with a production that is on the edge of asking a child to collaborate in imagery rendering the audience uncomfortable? A high-end example was performed in Manhattan in 2009. From the review of it, "A Relentless Wave Rolls in With an Inevitable Power," by Claudia La Rocco, in the *New York Times,* on June 11 of that year:

> Yet its cool surfaces thrum with simmering heat, as well as with often disturbing power dynamics and erotic undertones, particularly in one dramatically lighted section toward the end that features Greg Zucculo partnering the diminutive, terrifically spooky Allegra Herman, who is just 13 and wears an inscrutable, world-weary face, like something out of a Velázquez painting.
>
> Dressed in a high-necked black unitard, she seems in control, yet the duet ends with Mr. Zucculo carrying her, her head thrown back, into a narrow passageway behind the black paneled back wall. What fascinates here also repels, and Ms. Michelson is masterly in mining these tensions.

I, too, was present at this performance of the dance-theater work *Dover Beach,* discussed in La Rocco's review, and I can confirm that her prose nails its most unsettling episode. It was a strange, stomach-churning seventy-five minutes. Other children were involved. The subject had something to do with the mixed emotions adolescents feel in their obsessive studies of the ballet. Allegra Herman was awarded a Bessie for that performance, and the choreographer, Sarah Michelson, was named a fellow of the

MacArthur Foundation. Like the Viennese Children, the performances by the children in this production were polished to a fare-thee-well. An observer for whom painting is an interest may be moved to think of Balthus, so very controversial these days for his meticulous figurative canvases that show pre-adolescent girls posed with adult men so that a viewer glimpses their underpants. And yet, I wonder why Balthus is considered outré while Michelson is extolled. As for Allegra Herman, she has grown up to graduate from Columbia and to pursue a varied career as a professional dancer on stage and screen. In terms of her mental health, I can attest that when she was a student in my "Dance and Film" class at Barnard, she did brilliant and level-headed work. The fact that I didn't remember I had seen her in *Dover Beach* five or six years before I met her in class may be an indication that my own mental health—an inability to remember names—is in question. She was mesmerizing in that part. But was her youth being taken advantage of—or were our preconceptions about the representation of youth in art being tested?

In May 2009, the choreographer discussed the origins of her *Dover Beach* in *ArtForum International.* The interview, "1000 Words: Sarah Michelson," is a strong statement, including the information that her inspiration for this work, celebrated and controversial, was her visit to a few classes of unpromising little ballet girls and women in a small local studio in Wales, whose efforts Michelson watched for hours because she found the reason for them puzzling, given that they had the wrong bodies and, it seemed, no talent for ballet. She also notes that she included a reading aloud of Matthew Arnold's bleak love poem "Dover

Beach" in her work, even though its Romanticism disgusted her. As far as I can tell from her *ArtForum* comment, the emotion of the poem seemed appropriate to her for the dance passions she supposed to motivate the children. Evoking one of Arnold's images, she writes, "Most of them were not naturals, to say the least, but they were very serious. I could have watched it forever, these little girls throwing themselves up against this archetype in the middle of nowhere, for nobody." She relates then how she decided to make a piece where the performers are siloed from their own history as dancers. "For my own choreographic control, I'm struggling to eliminate a certain history of the dancer's body, the part that comes through rhythm or a performer's interpretation of how you get from one thing to the next. In this dance, I'm trying to create performers from scratch; I'm attempting to own and objectify them."

Michelson's thoughts, given the version of *Dover Beach* that was performed at New York's Chelsea theater the Kitchen, in 2009, are not uninteresting—part entomologist, part Doctor Moreau. The impersonality, somewhere between cool and cold, is fascinating. It has been shared, one surmises, by the greatest choreographers as well, and by great artists in other fields. As Martha Graham was quoted to have said, with professional intimacy, to Paul Taylor, regarding the Robert Rauschenberg head-to-toe-no-skin-showing costumes for Taylor's early trio *Three Epitaphs,* "Naughty boy, we must not cover up their faces." The difference between Taylor and Michelson in this matter, though, is that Taylor, who had to keep a company together, always went on the record about his dancers as human beings, while Michelson, with the brute honesty of someone who would never have to deal with the creatures again, just let her disgust at their pitiful illusions hang out. She permits us to see how the sausages are made. As a reviewer, I was engaged by the intellectual provocation of Michelson's rough guide to *Dover Beach*. However, as the mother of a small daughter who took ballet class at a local studio, I was appalled. Most important, though, my daughter grew up to love ballet thanks to those early classes, even though she didn't become a dancer. And the poem springs up anew at every rereading, as if it had just been born.

2 walking and dancing

At the end of the 1990s, nearly a decade after the unification of East and West Germany, I did some editorial work for a monthly journal of dance then called *ballett international/tanz aktuell* and today known as *tanz*. The office was based in Berlin, and I was brought over from New York for a few days to meet the staff and learn what I was supposed to contribute. The city was hopping, open, intensely alive. One afternoon, the editor Hartmut Regitz asked me if I'd like to tour more of Berlin than the route from my hotel to the office, and he generously drove me to see some areas of what had been East Berlin as well the West. Knowing that I'm Jewish,

he asked if I'd like to see the site of what had been the first He-
brew school in the city, from the eighteenth century, and, nearby,
what had been Berlin's oldest Jewish cemetery, the Grosse Hamburger Strasse Cemetery, both in the former East Berlin. Today,
two decades later, I know that the cemetery was founded in 1672
and used as a Jewish cemetery until it was closed in 1827, its
5,900 square meters (a little less than the area of a football field)
having been filled up with nearly three thousand graves. At the
time I visited the site, however, I knew none of the metrics, only
that the place was a memorial.

In a letter to me from Germany, the researcher and translator
Esther Kontarsky gives a brief account of the graveyard since the
1940s: "Its historic graves were preserved until the Gestapo ordered the graves to be destroyed. Across the final resting place
of over 2,600 people, the Gestapo had splinter trenches made,
which were shored up with stones from destroyed gravestones.
This measure also destroyed the grave of Moses Mendelssohn.
The famous philosopher of the Enlightenment had been buried
in the Jewish cemetery in 1786. In the spring of 1945, bombed and
fallen soldiers were buried in several mass graves in the cemetery.
By the 1970s the Parks Department of East Berlin had hauled
away most of the remaining stones on the lot, along with the
wooden crosses marking the graves of those non-Jews who had
died in air raids. In this refurbishing of the site, a few pieces of
stone were consolidated into a marker of a sort."

When Hartmut stopped the car, I prepared myself to encounter a grim footprint of the Holocaust, yet that's not quite what I
found, at least not at first. Instead, he led me to a plain expanse

of grass, or perhaps grass and ivy, surrounded on three sides by evergreen shrubs and stately trees. It was around four o'clock in the afternoon, and the weather was temperate, with a slow wind that ran through the leaves as if it were counting them. All of a sudden, I had the sense that I'd seen a version of this before—in *1980*, one of the dance-theater productions by the late German choreographer Pina Bausch (1940–2009) for her company, Tanztheater Wuppertal. Bausch—a graduate of the Juilliard School, in New York, as well as of the venerable Folkwang School for Music, Dance, and Speech (or Theater), in Essen, in her native Germany—made works lasting several hours, and their individual sections (some were playlets, some actual dances, some rituals) are woven from dance and theater, abstraction and realism, movement and words, psychoanalysis and animal instinct, and from many emotions and moods, including disgust and bitter comedy. Still performed and toured internationally by Tanztheater Wuppertal, they are this side of postmodern circus and that side of secular mystery play, and they can hurtle from one emotion to another without a whistle-stop for logic.

Several film documentaries recount how the company of fiercely individual actor-dancers with whom Bausch herself worked contributed personal material (willingly or not) to her theatrical constructions, so easily did their performances ring true, and so piercingly was she able to spotlight each person's unique magnetism. Her work and wit often tickle her audiences to laughter, yet the humor is rarely the product of gags but is, rather, situational. One can find oneself chortling at anecdotes and skits whose themes, recounted on paper, are horrific and whose choreographed action progresses according to a dynamic of aggression, rupture, and lonely resolution, sometimes at the micro level of individual relationships and sometimes at the macro level of nations and centuries. Bausch's use of repetition to reveal and satirize history evokes for me the Marxian witticism that goes, roughly: first time tragedy, second time farce. However, as I trod the grass of the Berlin park that had once been densely seeded with graves, I wasn't thinking of her theatrical expertise or her intellectual game-playing; I was considering how the design for her *1980* anticipated this place for me and wondering why it did.

A central element of Bausch's artistic practice was her emphasis on reinventing the stage floor uniquely for each work. One production was performed on a stage carpeted in chrysanthemums, another on one flooded by water, another on one buried by a rampart of stones that had crashed to the ground. Her four-hour-long *1980* was a spectacle whose broken throughline seemed to me, the one time I saw it live in the theater, to keep spiraling back to childhood, its traumas and absurdities and touches of receding magic. This work was performed on a stage cushioned by emerald turf; in one distant corner stood a life-sized model of a deer to which none of the performers paid visible attention. This Peter Pabst stage design, like most of Pabst's designs for Bausch over the quarter century he served as her collaborator, gave almost everything that took place on it a kind of coherence, even when the mood changed. Now a field, now a carpet, now a storybook symbol of the earth, it offered the audience, sometimes with unexpected emotional power, a comfortingly reliable foundation for the peculiar, illogical events that took place on it.

For me, Bausch's unique stage surfaces, each a challenge to herself requiring unique choreographic approaches, comprise her most profound theatrical statements concerning her engagement with the art and practice of theatrical dance and the scripted performance practice known as tanztheater.

That green carpet was the central image of my strobelike flashbacks to *1980* as Hartmut and I walked, yet it didn't calm my increasing uncertainty of what steps I should literally take. Was this sacred ground? Were there any bones left beneath the plantings? How many levels of consciousness and remembrance was I morally required to keep in play as we trod the field, as slowly as surveyors? Hartmut said little, and there was no signage at that time to educate a tourist's understanding of exactly what this was—just the grass and the trees and the wind and the day falling down. Eventually, I spotted what seemed to be a construction over toward one side of the field. Drawing closer, I could see that it was made of stones, a waist-high crazy quilt of mismatched remnants and smithereens, which had once belonged to entire grave markers, all somehow glued together, some bits with carved letters or dates, some with sculptural fragments. In the middle was a stone with a complete name. One name: it stood for all the names of all the former graves. Drawing close enough to read it, I froze: that representative turned out to be the name of a scholar I'd grown up being told was one of my mother's relatives, an eighteenth-century philosopher, political theorist, and full-hearted adherent of the ecumenical German Enlightenment. Now, there he was, stone central, with fragments of eighteenth- and nineteenth-century Jewish Berlin clinging alongside.

The King James Version of the Bible speaks of "walking" with God, in the sense of being at one with divinity. Unredeemed agnostic that I am, I was walking with my colleague and the wind. But the fact that I can write about this experience at all with any dispassion—crucial to reporting the recollection, as best I can, as nonfiction—is because my emotions had been prepared, rehearsed, by Bausch's *1980*. Still, what about it, apart from the stage design, had prepared me? To address that question, I recently watched an abbreviated archival film of a performance of the work that Tanztheater Wuppertal gave in 1984 in London at Sadler's Wells. Once again, I saw the man-child seated on a platform, spooning porridge into his mouth from an outsized, *Alice in Wonderland* bowl. I saw the adult trying to find a sleeping position and warmth under a child-size blanket. I saw the professional magician producing silks and living rabbits from thin air. I saw the skit with the performers crushed against one another in a lineup, now enacting an audition, now a collection of victims being belly-knifed seriatim, each with his or her own scream as unique as a fingerprint. Yet there were two elements I'd quite forgotten. One was a ritual procession of the smiling (or smirking) performers, costumed in evening dress, "speaking" in silent, enigmatic gestures as they paced the aisles of the theater in a regulated walk—a train of human beings without a destination, only a steady tempo. The other element I rediscovered, at the very end of *1980*, was a tableau in which the company—tall and short, young and middle-aged, no two physiques alike—lined up along three sides of the stage's green perimeter. Eureka! *They* were what had given me the sense of déjà vu: *They were what I felt*

I saw fifteen years later, transformed into the trees and shrubs lining the Grosse Hamburger Strasse Cemetery.

Furthermore, I discovered at this viewing that their very tableau was an intended memorial within the scene. After the film of *1980* had ended, before the credit crawl, the screen carried the note that *1980* was dedicated to Rolf Borzik. Who was that? I looked up the name and found he had been Bausch's beloved original designer and offstage partner in the 1970s and that this was the first spectacle Bausch made following his death, earlier in 1980, at the age of thirty-six—a terrible blow to her. The production—which I thought was potpourri surrealism when I saw it live in 1984 without having read the program—began to fall into place as a logically ordered elegy. The fragments of Shakespeare's lamenting Willow Song for Desdemona ("My true love he is gone"), sung intermittently, made sense; so did the plaintive comparison of two recorded performances by Judy Garland of "Over the Rainbow"—one from Garland's tremulous youth and the other from her throbbing maturity. Had I excavated this mourner's context from memory on that Berlin afternoon? Did the walk through the cemetery serve to unveil distant grief I'd witnessed in the theater, leading me to open myself to a sensation of grief for once-real individuals who were literally only names to me? Is one reason dance can be said to matter that it offers the possibility of serving as a theater of memory—of identity?

Looking back on what I've just written, I recall an early story by Isaac Babel titled, in Max Hayward's translation, "You Must Know Everything." The effects of dancing can be simple; indeed, dancing only matters at any given moment when it connects simply and directly with the practitioner or observer. However, to say anything cogent in retrospect about that connection in time and space can require a lifetime of study sometimes, and even at the end of the lifetime the study can prove destructive in other ways. (In the Babel story, the line, "You must know everything!" is uttered by a character who, as the novelist George Saunders has observed, doesn't have a clue that her husband's effort to realize the command literally led to his downfall.) Or perhaps the lesson is that living fully, dynamically, in the moment, is the most experience one can have, as with dance—an art of process, in which one continually strives to seize a quality (perfection of form, untiring energy, spiritual flow, endless exploration of physical possibility) that is only useful as an ideal because it cannot be grasped.

The man I thought was my mother's ancient relative was Moses Mendelssohn, and he was the kind of humanist who was always debating matters of a philosophical nature, although much more densely stated. Born in Dessau, in 1729, he died in Berlin, in 1786, in bed, perhaps from a cold in conjunction with a congenital ailment. Although he enjoyed early tutelage in the Talmud, mathematics, and one or two other basic subjects from his father (an impoverished copier of Torah scrolls); from David Fraenkel, the rabbi of Dessau and then of Berlin; and a few other mentors who recognized his intellectual gifts, he seems to have been largely self-taught in German literature, advanced Latin, Greek, French, Italian, philosophy, and the arts. He grew up to become a close friend of and co-editor with the Enlightenment playwright and theorist Gottfried Lessing, to win first prize from the Berlin Academy for an essay applying mathematical proofs to metaphysics in a competition where Immanuel Kant came in second, and to found Berlin's first public school for Jewish boys. Called by some of his colleagues in philosophy "the Jewish Socrates," his embrace of reason as the basis of faith and the route to knowledge of God contributed to the movement for Jews to assimilate themselves into Protestant German culture. He was so persuasive that, of his six children, four converted away from Judaism, including his son Abraham, the father of the composers Felix and Fanny Mendelssohn, who were brought up as Protestants. (All of the children who chose to convert waited to do so until after their father's death.) Among the subjects of their grandfather's many writings were essays on aesthetics of the literary and performing arts, the spiritual importance of human feeling, and rarefied topics in metaphysics, religion, and politics, which, to explicate, would surely require assistance from one of the overcoated angels in *Wings of Desire* (1987), the Wim Wenders film about spirituality in postwar Berlin. I give you a bit of the philosopher's biography since his name was the only one left to represent thousands of souls, now nameless, whose spirits undergirded my walk over what had once been their graves.

Around 2007, I learned recently, the Jewish cemetery was reconstructed once more, with a new stone marker for Moses Mendelssohn. I've never seen that one for real. Photographs show it to be a fine, classic tablet, but although its design is certainly in keeping with the dignity and stylistic period of the philosopher for whom it was fashioned, to me the rough, broken one it replaced was more appropriate, more eloquent, the painful jumble serving as a reminder that the bones the marker was meant to mark had been dug up and disposed of helter-skelter. Then again, as a one-time visitor, what gives me the right even to have an opinion on such a momentous issue of style? In fact, I recently learned also that my mother may not have been related to Moses Mendelssohn at all, that her father spent a little time in Germany as a teenager but was born and reared from a line of rabbis in Lithuania—that there is nothing special about me in this context, where, at best, I am no more nor less than a tourist, a kibitzer, self-appointed like any other critic.

Although I've never had the occasion to return to Germany in person, thanks to literature, journalism, and the performing arts, I continue to revisit remotely. I've also learned much more about Pina Bausch, enough to prompt me to respect her art and even, sometimes, enjoy it. A tutor in this regard was Wim Wenders, who decided to make a 3-D film, with a 2-D edition, about Bausch's artistry, embarking on it just as she died of cancer. Wenders wanted to abort the filming, but the company, grief-stricken, insisted he complete it; regardless of what you think of Bausch's work, this film, released in 2011, is outstanding, one of the finest memorials to a dancer of any kind. Representative scenes from four examples of her oeuvre are performed by her company in outdoor and indoor locations around the coal-mining area of Wuppertal, and in the context of everyday life and available light they look new, acquiring both an unfamiliar aura and a heroic authority. The walking procession from *1980* is performed by day on the top of a high hill or small mountain, and the fact that this train never reaches a visible terminus is neither surreal nor satirical there: it is life itself.

I once read an interview with a hard-working ballerina in which she said that if she ever had to travel more than a block in the city, she took a cab. Ballerinas—like medical personnel, police on the beat, employees of the food industry, and other front-line essential workers who protect your body, help maintain your well-being, or nurture your soul—are on their feet much of the day and, often, the evening; cabs (real and wished-for) make sense for them. However, absent an impeding physical ailment, one isn't likely to hear a writer echo the ballerina. Apart from the rare users of a standing desk, writers tend to spend most of a working day planted on the keister, and after several hours of trying to sweat out a few verses, walking is a kind of treat, even a demonstration of pride that one is still capable of action in fact, as well as in imagining.

Early in this century, I took a memorable walk through one neighborhood of Harlem with the dancer Lowell Smith. To appreciate its effect on me requires a little background. I had met Lowell some thirty years before, in the mid-1970s, when he had just joined the Dance Theatre of Harlem, and the company was in residence as part of the Dance Magnet program at Jefferson High School in Portland, Oregon, where I was reporting on dance for the local alternative paper *Willamette Week*. Arthur Mitchell, the company's co-founder and driving force, invited me to observe a DTH rehearsal of George Balanchine's *Serenade,* which was taking place there. Lowell—a superb dramatic dancer with excellent classical training via North Carolina School of the Arts and the Joffrey Ballet School—was not built for Balanchine. Although he was tall (six feet), he was heavily muscled and barrel-chested, and at DTH he was rarely cast in "white-tights roles" (leading-man parts). However, ballerinas attested to the fact that he was a strong and reliable partner; he had soaring elevation; and he lived in music as if he'd written it.

At this rehearsal of *Serenade,* Lowell was, uncustomarily, given a leading role as the artist figure in the "Elegy" at the end. During that section, he had the chance to perform one great leap at Balanchine's behest in concert with Tchaikovsky, and he seized the moment, bounding ceilingward as if he'd been saving the leap for his entire life, as if his body was singing the action—a sudden intake of breath, a holding of the high note longer than seemed humanly possible, and a magically restrained descent. I never saw any other dancer in that part match the grandeur of expression Lowell exacted from that moment of the rehearsal; it forever opened a window on an aspect of *Serenade* of which I hadn't been conscious—offered the possibility that the male figure, like the ballerina, had an interior life teeming with (in the words of poet Kenneth Koch) wishes, lies, and dreams.

During the DTH residency in Portland I met and interviewed Lowell; and when he was invited back on his own to teach there by Mary Folberg, the dance program's founder, I observed his class. I often saw him on stage with DTH in New York during his seventeen-year tenure with the company, too, admiring his impassioned Hilarion in *Giselle*—typecasting of Lowell by the genetic luck of the draw, which accorded him the physique of a heavyweight boxer rather than Albrecht's dashing fencer—along with his Stanley Kowalski in Valerie Bettis's *Streetcar Named Desire,* a figure out of Greek tragedy updated in a wifebeater; and his sorrow-wise Pastor in Agnes de Mille's *Fall River Legend.*

The walk: So, around 2006, I went up to West 152nd Street to attend a Sunday afternoon demonstration by the Dance Theatre of Harlem at which Lowell was present. At the end, I went up to him to say hello, and we left together, strolling south on Broadway to catch a downtown train. Lowell spoke about his dissatisfaction with his opportunities for teaching at that time; he wasn't happy. Hoping to elevate his mood a little, I asked him if he remembered the *Serenade* rehearsal at Jefferson High. Brightening, he answered that he did. I told him again how remarkable I thought he was in it, especially the leap. He recalled that it had felt special to him as well. "Where did the leap come from?" I asked. He understood that I was asking whether the action was something he planned or whether it burst from that state of energized focus that is sometimes called flow. He couldn't say, at least to me, and he didn't try to make up an explanation. Sometimes there are no explanations; sometimes the art of dance isn't reasonable. Or fair: that's when I learned that he wasn't often cast in Balanchine ballets, much as he admired them. He had the training and experience for some Balanchine parts, and he had the courage and sophistication and certainly the musicality, but he didn't look right in the choreography: his limbs and back didn't make the severe lines that brought out the mysterious geometry of Balanchine's thinking. Although body problems in ballet are frequently associated with women, Lowell was the first performer to make clear to me the heartache over one's inherited physicality that men in ballet can also suffer.

A decade later, I was introduced to several dancers who were completing their final year at the School of American Ballet. They had just finished performing in the annual workshop, so I had seen them all dance and knew how accomplished each was. One handsome young man, a very long drink of water, whose dancing showed a fine style and elegant carriage in the performance, as well as the right musculature for princely roles, was downcast at the reception. I asked him if something was the matter, and he said that it was explained to him that he was too tall to join a prominent professional company. His parents were willing to support him to go to college, and that is what he intended to do. He knew how lucky he was to have the option of college; still, the foreclosure of his dance dream was a blow.

As I wrote this, at the end of 2020, the entire art form of ballet worldwide was full of anxiety about foreclosed dreams. In a virtual repertory program on line from Seattle's Pacific Northwest Ballet, one could watch an intermission feature of a conversation between the company's artistic director, Peter Boal, and the choreographer Twyla Tharp, an excerpt of whose *Waterbaby Bagatelles* PNB performs with panache. Boal explained to Tharp that, thanks to the virtual offerings of the company that season, he was hoping they could bring in two million dollars in earned income. But Boal's brow was deeply furrowed: ordinarily, in the late fall *Nutcracker* season, PNB brings in twenty-five million in earned income. Peter Boal had been a principal dancer at the New York City Ballet before he took over the direction of the Seattle company. He began to study ballet at SAB at the right age and grew up to have the right proportions and musculature—as well as the turnout and refined technique—for the plum male parts in the repertories of Balanchine and Robbins. In this interview, though, his past glory, plus a couple of dollars, at best might get one of his fans a cup of coffee. He couldn't say where the company he leads was going to muster the funds to have a future, and he didn't try to make up an explanation.

That walk to the subway with Lowell around 2006 was the last time I saw him. The next time I encountered his name was in a *New York Times* obituary, in 2007: he had died of lung cancer, prematurely, at age fifty-six. Arthur Mitchell himself, the company's co-founder, had alerted the newspaper. "He was the type of male classical dancer you don't see anymore," Mitchell said. "He had a presence." The obit also quoted Lowell's point of view from the inside. "Ballet shows you there is an absolute right," he told the *Detroit Free Press*. "There is only one way."

What does it take to turn a walk into a dance? There are certainly partnered dances that are variations on walking: the one-step, the Castle Walk, the foxtrot, the Argentine tango, the polonaise. The cakewalk usually has some actual walking in it (that is, a progression of the walker through alternation of the legs at a steady pace with one foot fully on the floor each time and no loft of the body between steps), but the ragtime-era films of cakewalkers show them typically to use the dance as a way to launch themselves into strutting and idiosyncratic variations on perambulation. (The great Bert Williams gives a fantastical example in the cakewalking episode of the Biograph silent feature *Lime Kiln Field Day* of 1913, believed to be the oldest known feature film to feature African American actors.) But what purpose do these walking dances serve that a companionable walk—or an athletic trot or run—might not? If you can walk, you can dance; but why does it matter to dance if dancing is not one's profession? Why doesn't simply walking to music, or without it, suffice? What is the impetus that transports walking into dancing?

In his two volumes on the history of beauty—Beauty—as an idea, ideal, philosophical principle, and lodestar for the senses as well as for the mind, from the Venus of Willendorf of the thirtieth millennium BCE to Twiggy in the 1970s, Umberto Eco lays bare the multifaceted thinking on the subject in the Western world. The philosopher Elaine Scarry, in her provocative essay "On Beauty and Being Wrong" (contained with the title essay in the volume *On Beauty and Being Just* of 1999), anatomizes how one recognizes the beautiful, in life and in art. I feel very lucky to have found these marvelous books, for they rescued me from the uncomfortably specific definition of beauty I'd been holding on to since the mid-1970s, when the esteemed art historian Ernst Gombrich came to lecture in Portland, Oregon. I was assigned to speak with him by *Willamette Week,* and as the sole journalist who asked for an interview, I was given an entire hour alone with him to discuss aesthetics. Gombrich told me that there was one paradigm worldwide for beauty in human beings, a series of relationships for elements of the face and the body as based on the golden section, first described in the writings of Euclid, which uses a mathematical procedure and geometry to show why symmetry in nature and in art pleases the eye and to explain the artist's journey as a search for this specific perfection.

Gombrich's reflections can be quite helpful in discussing international court dances, including many of Africa and Asia, as well as classical and neoclassical ballet and nearly all European folk dances. However, they aren't relevant to such artists as the unflaggingly inventive flamenco star Rocío Molina, whose rhythmic brilliance not only rivals that of the pre–World War II flamenco genius Carmen Amaya but who also invents unforeseen new full-body movement, such as leaps that take her down to the floor as if she'd been shot, or her use of the train of flamenco's most fancy, bata de cola dress as a brake to her furious impetus when, whirlwind fashion, she rolls in the dress on the ground— all while sustaining a companionate pulse to the cantaor and clapping musicians who accompany her dance. This is not a search for perfection, that is, for full control of one's action: it is an immersion in letting go. Even if the structure of the dance has been decided in advance, the glory of it is that it looks as if the dancer is making it up on the spot. Molina is lovely in repose, and she can be a real cut-up, too; but while dancing she is never pretty, and her comedy entirely derives from her dance movement rather than from character; she is majestic, monumental, supernatural, and thanks to Umberto Eco, I feel comfortable adding that, for me, she is beautiful.

In his *History of Beauty* (2004), Eco provides a third-century quotation from Plotinus that justifies using the term "beauty" to refer to Molina, or to such asymmetrical and questing movement artists as Eiko Otake. Eiko became world-famous as part of the team Eiko and Koma, with her husband, the painter Koma, now seemingly retired from dance. In recent years, Eiko has partnered with other collaborators and also performed alone, yet her principled art, driven by grief for what we have visited upon the earth, has not changed significantly in its mission in the thirty-five years I've been a member of its audience. Her movement consists of what look like countless transformations of energy among muscles and tendons, resulting in the repositioning of her body at a glacial pace and always in remarkable settings (a spectacular man-made forest, a piano in a graveyard, a river, train stations). By millimeters, or inchingly, she tours a room or an outdoor sidewalk, lies down, shifts position, stands, touches something, turns away. She creates a strange suspense for those with whom her work connects, the kind of suspense you feel when you aren't sure if it's going to pour and you have to calculate whether to run home and get protective clothing.

When Eiko was younger, her exquisite body would often be naked in performance; these days, she is clothed, usually in a kimono, her gestures and halting advances becoming elements of what is meant by "Nature." For audience members with patience and willingness to submit to the experience of watching her, she can alter an onlooker's internal clock and expectations so as to call attention to larger forces—time as measured by light or temperature change, space as measured by whether it is filled with or absent a body, and, since Eiko's is a tragic art, dark deterioration as measured by the foreclosure of possibility. (An example of the last is Eiko's video-and-installation project *A Body in Fukushima,* with scholar William Johnston, who filmed and photographed her journeying on foot with her billowing, pigeon-blood-red companion cloth in full silent cry. The film was made during their five elegiac trips to the area, beginning in 2011, across that unlucky region of Japan devastated by a trifecta of earthquake, tsunami, and nuclear meltdown.)

Here is how Eco's Plotinus reads, from "On the Intellectual Beauty" in his *Fifth Ennead:* "In truth there is no beauty more authentic than the wisdom we find and love in some individual. We should leave aside his face, which may be ugly, nor should we pay any heed to his appearance, but look for his inner beauty. But if that [inner beauty] does not move you to call such a man beautiful, when you look inside yourself you will not perceive yourself as beautiful either." In other words, in contrast to obvious visual beauty, by which one is ineluctably struck—the way the beauty of Nausicaa, for instance, as Elaine Scarry reminds the reader, stops Odysseus in his tracks—the interior beauty that Plotinus describes must be sought, uncovered, regardless of the subject's physical appearance. Eiko is a paradigm of Plotinus's observations.

As I write, there are efforts in the United States and Europe to make this second type of beauty a priority above appearance for conventional ballet as well, as in the Dutch National Ballet production *Coppelia,* televised in 2021: part live, part animated, with a new score by Maurizio Malagnini and new choreography by company artistic director Ted Brandsen. The story has been reconceived so that Doctor Coppelius is a fiendish cosmetic surgeon who wants to remove the townspeople's individuality. Their brave rescuer, named Swan, is danced by Michaela DePrince, formerly of the DNB and now a soloist with the Boston Ballet. DePrince has a heart-catching backstory herself, and one would have to be Madame Defarge to ignore her interview pleas for dancers not to be typecast or stereotyped, that is, to dance straightforwardly as themselves, regardless of whether the woman in the pas de deux towers over the man or whether, as in DePrince's case, a skin condition (vitiligo) is allowed to be seen fully, unmasked by makeup.

The DNB production has ingenious aspects, especially in the melding of live-action and animation, and DePrince and each of her colleagues (a group that includes a finely trained Daniel Camargo as Frantz, an enthusiastic Vito Mazzeo as the villainous Doctor C, and, larger-than-life in cameo parts, the erstwhile Royal Ballet stars Darcey Bussell and Irek Mukhamedov) works like a Trojan to put over the concept. But some things had to be sacrificed: the original score by Léo Delibes, a masterpiece; the choreography and beloved mime roles, as inherited from one of the nineteenth-century productions in Russia or Denmark or from a Ballet Russe company; all evidence of petit allégro and shading of the upper body, so that the language of ballet is severely restricted to pirouettes and high legs; and perhaps most saddening, any visible links to the ballet's origins and long performance tradition: even the title, *Coppelia,* has lost the accent aigu over the "e" (and, with it, the reminder that the first production—one of ballet's rare long-lived comedies about village life without a royal or an aristocrat in sight—was given during the Siege of Paris in the Franco-Prussian War in 1870).

The nineteenth- and twentieth-century international ballet repertoire is undergoing similar reconsideration in many companies, and one is also reminded of the hard choices that Agrippina Vaganova and her colleagues were forced to make in the USSR in order to preserve the classic ballets in some form, given Stalin's emphasis on narrative works whose stories would have immediate relevance to Soviet ideals. I and my generation have no skin in this game: it is up to my daughter's and granddaughter's generations to decide what to retain from the past. Yet, I do caution that decisions being made now to revise historic repertoires according to the principles of interior beauty alone, as understood by today's cultural standards, may irreparably damage the exterior beauty that kept these works alive for more than a century.

So far in this section, I have been looking at ballet and dance from the point of view of its practitioners. I now take a hairpin turn and go shoulder to shoulder with my fellow audience members, the vast majority of whom will have in common a predilection for and a lifelong knowledge of walking. Dancers or not, a core expenditure of physical energy shared by those on stage and those seated to watch them is the act of walking.

Walking intensifies consciousness of oneself in space. If you're walking with someone else, the physical proximity between the two of you in the course of traveling can intensify the intimacy of a conversation. If you're prone to meditative moods, walking as a solitary can prompt conceptual thinking or free up the brain for a Eureka moment, or even an epiphany. Miraculously, with a little bounce between steps, it can jog the memory. A few bio-logical reasons for this—such as the increased circulation of the blood prompted by a weight-bearing activity whose controlled pace makes it still possible to gather together one's mental forces on a topic outside the physical action (necessary, for instance, in the writing of an entire book in one's head en route, as Friedrich Nietzsche claimed to have done while walking)—are deftly un-packed by Ferris Jabr in his *New Yorker* fact story of September 3, 2014, "Why Walking Helps Us Think."

The *New Yorker*'s contributors and editors have always been a thinking bunch, and several generations of them have pondered the act of walking—in particular, walking around and through New York City—from every conceivable angle during the nearly a century of the magazine's existence. Jabr's column is one of at least three that the *New Yorker* published on aspects of walking between the falls of 2013 and 2014 alone. Another of those stories is "A Walker in the City," Joshua Rothman's profile from Sep-tember 17, 2013, of William Helmreich, a professor of sociology and a New York native, who, at the time of the profile's publica-tion, had walked 120,000 blocks in the five boroughs over the preceding four years, thereby earning his title claim in his then-latest volume, *The New York Nobody Knows* (2013). And in Au-gust 25, 2014, staff writer Adam Gopnik wrote a brilliant "Critic at Large" article called "Heaven's Gaits: What We Do When We Walk." It opens: "Why people walk is a hard question that looks easy." Gopnik chronicles a pair of books on facets of the history of walking in Europe and the United States, including the bizarre competitive-walking events in the United States and, in opposition, the walking crawls of the dandies through the great cities of Europe. Perhaps in the spirit of James Thurber, Gopnik takes note of how the presence of small children impedes a walking routine and concludes that, as life winds down, so does the energy to take long walks, leading back to the writer's penchant for sitting and, eventually, to the ultimate supine position in the casket, in which the once-a-walker is carried out of the world feet first.

A slightly more conventional historian of urban walking is the British author Matthew Beaumont, whose collection of essays, *The Walker: On Losing and Finding Yourself in the Modern City* (2020), is described as "a literary history of walking from Dickens to Žižek." Beaumont's previous literary walkathon, *Nightwalking: A Nocturnal History of London* (2016), offers a competitor to the New York completist Professor Helmreich in the redoubtable athlete Captain Barclay (Robert Barclay Allardice). In 1809, on a bet, the game captain walked a thousand miles, in a thousand hours, for a thousand guineas. Thirty-two pounds lighter, he made the bet, presumably settled whatever debts of his were in the red, visited a cobbler and a comfortable armchair, and then, eight days later, suited up in his captain's uniform and joined the British military to fight Napoleon, who was famously painted five times in four years, by Jacques-Louis David, in transit across the Alps on the back of a horse who did the walking.

There's more to literary walking, though, than putting one foot in front of the other: there's the speculation of why walking matters. One example was provided by Honoré de Balzac, who published a theory of walking, in French, as the essay "Théorie de la démarche," in 1833. He spoke there of walking as a way to discover "the physiognomy of the body" by studying individual gaits. The Russian scholar Daria Khitrova has referred to Balzac's ideas in the essay as "tongue in cheek" and "ironic," although Ralph Waldo Emerson seemed to take it seriously when he noted that its French publication had, by a dozen years, preceded the publication of an essay by another transcendentalist that Emerson much admired. Balzac's essay has never been translated into English: there's a good project for the humanities—see if the irony pervades the English version, with notes and a contextual essay!

In the event, until the Balzac is available in English, I declare that, in my experience, the laurel for bringing into print the most eloquent and continuously surprising essay on the subject belongs to the *Atlantic Monthly,* which, in June 1862, published the lecture called "Walking" (or "The Wild"). Its posthumous author, Henry David Thoreau, had worked on the text steadily in between the many times he delivered it as a lecture to men's clubs over the better part of the preceding decade. In the published version—an ode to the essay form itself, from its overarching scaffold of logical argument to support the point of how walking will reinvigorate wild Nature and thereby save the world, to the welter of images buoying up individual sentences—walking is represented as a chivalric pilgrimage by self-making gentlemen. As long as the walker can rely on a washerwoman (or his mother) to do the laundry and, perhaps, whip up some yams for dinner, walking promises emancipation from the constrictions of culture to pursue a vision of Nature uninfected by mankind. Thoreau's reason to attempt the pilgrimage, literally and figuratively, is to maintain the health of the earth. Perhaps the most memorable line in the lecture reads, "In Wildness is the preservation of the World," a phrase that, during the environmental movement blossoming in the late 1960s and 1970s, could, in all earnestness, be found on the bumper stickers of gas-guzzling cars.

For all the irony, many other powerfully melodious lines are worth remembering. Thoreau's lecture is a paean to an encompassing ideal, a plan for his audiences' literal transportation (how gentlemen could live right now) and spiritual transportation (how they should live in the near future: an ideal equating wildness with the condition of literal freedom where, among other things, there would be "no fugitive slave laws"). Thoreau, who practiced the art of poetry from time to time (he tucked one of his own smartly metered ruminations into the final draft of "Walking"), does not forget aesthetics: "In literature, it is only the wild that attracts us. Dullness is but another name for tameness." Although the linking of Thoreau and dance is infrequently found in the same sentence, one rare example was written by the artist Joseph Cornell, in his introductory comment to the issue of Lincoln Kirstein's periodical *Dance Index* titled *Americana—Romantic Ballet* (vol. 6, no. 9 [1947]). "A metaphysical musing on ballet by Melville would be a welcome find," Cornell writes. "And after coming upon a poem inspired by the subject in such a 'recluse' as Emily Dickinson ("I Cannot Dance Upon My Toes"), it might not be too surprising to stumble across some lines of the hermit of Walden, similarly preoccupied."

Cornell himself was an inveterate walker; he liked to take the subway from his family's home on Utopia Parkway, in Queens, to the East River side of Manhattan's 42nd Street, then to spend the day making his way on foot to the Hudson River at the west end of the street. This peregrination would be punctuated by frequent stops into the little stores lining the sidewalk during the 1930s and 1940s, to browse through and buy books and prints and beads and tchotchkes of many kinds for his astonishing, magical shadow boxes and collages, a number of which were homages to the Real Ballerinas of History, from Marie Taglioni to Allegra Kent. When Cornell, an artist of exquisite taste and imagination, chose a ballerina as a subject of one of his art works, it was an all-American conferral of an Order of Chivalry. It would have gone without saying for followers of *Dance Index,* where he suggested the linking of Melville and Thoreau with ballet, that the suggestion was intended to be a compliment to Melville and Thoreau.

I don't know of any twentieth-century essay in English on walking that comes up to the standard of Thoreau's rhetorical mastery and poetic suggestiveness. What I'd offer instead as a match is the obverse design, by Adolph Alexander Weinman, of the Walking Liberty half dollar, a New World goddess in a long, lightly pleated empire gown, the American flag draped over one shoulder, her left arm cradling fresh branches and her right arm gesturing forward to the rising sun toward which she strides, left leg leading, back monumentally placed, sculptural neck supporting her perfectly shaped head with its upswept hair and exquisite profile worth being struck on a coin. (In fact, Weinman's Walking Liberty, minted from 1916 to 1947, and his Mercury dime, minted from 1916 to 1945, seem to have enjoyed the same model for the faces: a bust he made, in 1913, of young Elsie Stevens, wife of the poet and attorney Wallace Stevens. The model for Walking Liberty's vigorous, high-breasted body has not been definitively identified, although it seems quite possibly to have been the tall, rangy model Audrey Munson.) This design—evoking the Nike of Samothrace, the more delicate and psychically complex Sower of art nouveau medalist Louis-Oscar Roty, and, in several respects, Augustus Saint-Gaudens's Diana of 1893—has been cited by specialists in numismatics as the most gazable U.S. coin minted in the past hundred years, regardless of who is looking down at it. Weinman, an immigrant from Germany, studied sculpture with Saint-Gaudens, among others, at Cooper Union. Had he ever seen the young Isadora Duncan? One instep of Walking Liberty is clearly shown in the design: it is high, like Duncan's. Yet even if the sculptor hadn't had a dancer in mind, the figure is invested with graceful motion—because of the vigor of her stride, the placement of her spine and lighthouse-beam strength of her head, and the windswept, wild disposition of the fabric she wears and carries. The combination of strength, elegance, and mission, which can be found in the essay form itself ("a mental stroll," as essayist Phillip Lopate has called the essay genre) and that characterizes Thoreau's "Walking," too, can also, I submit, be found in Walking Liberty, along with the balletic possibilities that Cornell divined in Melville and Thoreau.

Transportation and transcendence, concepts familiar to students of American literature of the 1860s, were embedded around the same time in literature of England and France, though not quite in the same spirit. In mid-nineteenth-century Paris, just after the decade of spectacular Romantic ballets at the Opéra (the "Ballet of the Nuns," *La Sylphide, Giselle*) during the 1830s and 1840s, there developed a cultural figure in common parlance and in fact who represented a particular kind of walker, a *flâneur*. This was a stroller or observer, often dandified, with no particular purpose or destination in walking, save to experience the city, a reporter sans assignment who sometimes made verbal snapshots of urban life in personal essays of description and reflection, marked by irony or even cynicism. The flâneurs (and, on occasion, the odd *flâneuse*) attended the ballet; post-impressionist painters found them, the *-eurs* top-hatted, approaching the dancing girls from behind as the dancers waited to make their stage entrances from the wings. The literary profile of this kind of walker—lured on by his limitless appetite for urban novelties made possible by the Industrial Revolution, and now and then chastened by his vestigial attachments to a rapidly vanishing pastoral environment— is attributed to several writers of the period, perhaps most prominently the Second Empire poet Charles Baudelaire. Glancing backward today, the flâneur's world pops up as a kaleidoscope of impressions and impressionists, of vision arrested by photography, of locomotives and gaslight and the scintillating ephemera of sawdust and tinsel, the racecourse, the ballet, of dance halls and absinthe and electricity, of magnetism and microbes, TB and syphilis. Above all, it was a world in motion, a round-the-clock entertainment of living surfaces for the delectation of . . . You, Monsieur Flâneur, aesthete, dandy, stroller, boulevardier detached from everything and everything on offer to your insatiable gaze.

In 1863, a year after the *Atlantic Monthly* published Thoreau's

"Walking," a paean to the country, Baudelaire published, in the Parisian newspaper *Le Figaro,* his portrait of the walker in the city, a godlike onlooker who is everywhere present and nowhere visible (here in Jonathan Mayne's translation):

> The crowd is his element, as the air is that of birds and water of fishes. His passion and his profession are to become one flesh with the crowd. For the perfect *flâneur,* for the passionate spectator, it is an immense joy to set up house in the heart of the multitude, amid the ebb and flow of movement, in the midst of the fugitive and the infinite. To be away from home and yet to feel oneself everywhere at home; to see the world, to be at the center of the world, and yet to remain hidden from the world—impartial natures which the tongue can but clumsily define. The spectator is a prince who everywhere rejoices in his incognito. The lover of life makes the whole world his family, just like the lover of the fair sex who builds up his family from all the beautiful women that he has ever found, or that are or are not—to be found; or the lover of pictures who lives in a magical society of dreams painted on canvas. Thus the lover of universal life enters into the crowd as though it were an immense reservoir of electrical energy. Or we might liken him to a mirror as vast as the crowd itself; or to a kaleidoscope gifted with consciousness, responding to each one of its movements and reproducing the multiplicity of life and the flickering grace of all the elements of life.

The ballet and dance reviews of poet and novelist Théôphile Gautier do investigate the art of movement and theatrical presence and demonstrate considerable acuity in aesthetic evaluation; however, they seem to chime in with Baudelaire's flâneur often. Sometimes, the reason for gossipy asides or other additions of non-dancing subjects seems to be to give the reader relief from having to follow a dancer dancing and then to suffer the head-ache of precise assessment. Even impassioned music lovers and balletomanes cannot bear very much homing in on specific passages of music or dancing in the newspaper over morning coffee without the treat of the camera's pulling back to show the context of audience, politics, biography—of the surrounding world that doesn't require one to remember the difference between a pas de cheval and a pas de chat. By the twentieth century, though, thanks to the reviews of H. T. Parker in Boston, Carl Van Vechten and John Martin in the *New York Times,* Walter Terry in the *New York Herald Tribune,* and a few others, readers of dance reviews in the largest U.S. cities began to want more confirmation in print about what dancers they saw last night did in performance, or whether whatever they did was worthwhile. The critics were increasingly likely to be professional journalists or erstwhile actors or even dance historians or trained dancers themselves, and most of them actually tried to concentrate on stage events. Then came the internet, and with it went the jobs; why pay a critic to tell you what you think you know better? Of course, the internet brought much more information as well and made access to much of it for free. In the twenty-first century, dance critics are expected to weigh in on everything from trance dances to Tik-Tok. Lamentably, as the critics' responsibilities grow to become walking (or staggering) encyclopedias of the art, the number of forums open to them to review dance in a substantial way continues to diminish.

Fortunately, on both sides of the Atlantic, English-language readers who love dance have had worthy and interesting critics and historians going back well over a century. The following passage from "Dancers, Buildings, and People in the Street," an essay-lecture by Edwin Orr Denby (1903–1983)—dance critic, poet, choreographer, novelist, translator—brings together close looking at movement with a panoptic sweep of its social and cultural contexts (the essay, from 1954, is widely published, including in his collected *Dance Writings* from 1986). When Denby looks at people dancing, he goes beyond the steps they practice or how they relate to music or design. He considers what painters or photographers would call the negative space surrounding the person moving and the imaginative possibilities of how that space extends the mover's possible intentions and the movement's possibly unintended effects into the cultural surround:

Speaking personally, I think there is quite a difference between seeing people dance as part of daily life, and seeing them dance in a theater performance. Seeing them dance as part of daily life is seeing people dance in a living room or a ballroom or a night club, or seeing them dance folk dances either naturally or artificially in a folk dance group. For that matter classroom dancing and even rehearsal dancing seem to me a part of daily life, though they are as special as seeing a surgeon operate, or hearing the boss blow up in his office. Dancing in daily life is also seeing the pretty movements and gestures people make. In the Caribbean, for instance, the walk of Negroes is often, well, miraculous—both the feminine stroll and the masculine one, each entirely different. In Italy you see another beautiful way of strolling, that of shorter muscles, more complex in their plasticity, with girls deliciously turning their breast very slightly, deliciously pointing their feet. You should see how harmoniously the young men can loll. American young men loll quite differently, resting on a peripheral point; Italians loll resting on a more central one. Italians on the street, boys and girls, both have an extraordinary sense of the space they really occupy and of filling that space harmoniously as they rest or move. Americans occupy a much larger space than their actual bodies do; I mean, to follow the harmony of their movement or of their lolling you have to include a much larger area of space than they are actually occupying. This annoys many Europeans; it annoys their instinct of modesty. But it has a beauty of its own which a few of them appreciate. It has so to speak an intellectual appeal; it has because it refers to an imaginary space, an imaginary volume, not to a real and visible one. Europeans sense the intellectual volume, but they fail to see how it is filled with intellectual concepts—so the American they see lolling, and assuming to himself too much space, more space than he actually needs, is a kind of conqueror, is a kind of nonintellectual or merely material occupying power.

Denby's inventory of national walks (or national characters) isn't as persuasive in our century as it may have been in 1954, less than a decade after V-E Day, when this essay was new and the Cold War poured concrete on borders within nations as well as between them. So much has changed since, and Denby's classifications of walking according to national differences (the physical counterpoint in the bodies of walking Italians, the awkwardly tall Americans lolling, and so forth) seem like stereotypes from another age looked at with the scientific curiosity of Darwin among the songbirds. However, still inspiring are Denby's practices of closely observing people in motion on stage and off, for the pure pleasure of doing so, and his genius for using everyday language to describe both large patterns of crowds as if scanned from above and minute rhythmic play within the musculature of an individual moving body, as if studied from the closeness of an embrace.

He retained the teeming attentiveness of the flâneur while exchanging the assertiveness of self for Keatsian negative capability. One can reread his essays scores of times and still learn something new.

In 1983, between the deaths of Balanchine—Denby's hero—in April and of Denby himself, in July, New York City Ballet gave the premiere of *Glass Pieces* by Jerome Robbins, a storyless one-act ballet set to three works for orchestra by Philip Glass ("Rubric," "Façades," and excerpts from the opera *Akhnaten*). Running through each of the ballet's three sections is the theme of walking, articulated in each instance by the corps de ballet.

I've seen NYCB's production of *Glass Pieces* many times since the first performance, and for most of those years, I presumed that it was an embodiment—perhaps intentional, perhaps unconsciously—of themes in Denby's "Dancers, Buildings, and People in the Street." But presuming is related to understanding as browsing is related to reading: it's more than nothing but not good enough. Recently, I studied a film on YouTube of the Paris Opéra Ballet in *Glass Pieces*. Although the tempo is slower than the one I remember from live performances by NYCB, the choreography is carefully rendered, with devoted attention to detail. (Robbins was quite admiring of the way the Opéra performed his works, for good reason.) Studying the ballet with the opportunity to pause the film and rerun it as needed, I recognized choreographic elements I'd breezed over for years. And I realized that Robbins's vision of the walkers is actually in opposition to Denby's vision. Robbins and Denby complement one another, yet they do not agree.

In the first section, to a hectic theme for flutes and woods ob-sessively twisting up and down a scale, dancers in mismatched practice clothes stream out of each wing and cross the stage with purposeful direction, everyone locked into getting to the wing opposite, gaze magnetized by the goal. Their homogeneous walk is an undeviating, parallel-legged, heel-first pace; the look of the whole group is quite like how the Great Hall of Grand Central looks at a weekday rush hour when workers aren't kept home by a pandemic. (In a filmed interview that NYCB made with prin-cipal dancer Russell Janzen, we learn that the scores of perform-ers in this section are not given specific walking paths; should they collide, they have to rescue themselves spontaneously.) Sud-denly, in the midst of this human ant-farm—this cartoonish em-bodiment of commuters in the 1950s—wing in a pair of higher beings, each in a shining pastel unitard, who catapult themselves on stage with a curious, parallel-legged leap, taking off from one leg and landing on two. Unlike the pedestrians, these angelic im-migrants do not alternate their arms but rather hold them in a flying gymnastic carriage related to, yet also distinct from, the syllabus of classic dance. The woman of the pair wears pointe shoes, the dancers both stretch their limbs and point their toes in air, and the leap is reminiscent of a balletic assemblé without their looking as if they are in a ballet world: in this context, their leaps are related to the walking of the pedestrians through the common parallel position, although that shared physical element is elevated by these elite speakers into what Lincoln Kirstein once called the "aria of the aerial." The walkers clear out, and the aliens have a few moments to dance together by themselves. When alone together the first thing they do is to execute turned-out alternating lunge steps with alternating arms, that is, the balletic transformation of an everyday walk into the art of dance.

The pedestrians return, still negotiating rush hour, though this time with slight variations introduced into their walking—a sudden turn between two paces, a quick step to the side, a hiccough in the homogeneity. A second couple from beyond, also in gleaming unitards, enters leaping, and they, too, have an effect on the pedestrians, who introduce more turns or sudden, quick knee bends (evocative of balletic demi-pliés) and half-turns into their own pacing. Eventually, a third alien couple drops into rush hour, with further effect on the walkers and further transformational walk-evoking lunges. Each entrance is ushered in by a new musical statement. At one breathtaking moment, the pedestrians freeze in place—all taking the knee bend in strict profile; suddenly, measured against the glowing backdrop of crossing lines evoking graph paper, they momentarily are transformed into figures on ancient kraters. At the next crossover, the pedestrians add little details they've learned from the visitors plus a new one—raising one arm overhead. We are no longer in Grand Central or on a sidewalk; we're fully in the world of art. Eventually, the three alien couples band together downstage while the pedestrians are lined upstage, and the aliens begin to cross from wing to wing using the lunges that are the dance transformations of the original walk. Upstage, the pedestrians begin to copy them, learning how to become glorious aliens, that is, how to become dancers. The three couples disappear, and the pedestrians return to their crossing walks for a moment. Then the music cuts off and they freeze in place.

This transformation of stereotypical pedestrianism into dance as an art seems to have been a characteristic pursuit of Robbins over his career on the concert stage. For me, the outstanding example occurs in the first moments of *Dances at a Gathering,* an hour-long piano ballet to Chopin, where the character sometimes called, for his costume, the Boy in Brown (Edward Villella originally, and since always performed by virtuosos) walks meditatively onto the bare stage without any sound accompaniment. He surveys the space, then carefully crouches to place one full palm on the stage floor, as if it were a land he was returning to after a long absence. The pianist only begins to play Chopin's Mazurka op. 63, no. 3, when the performer stands and becomes a dancer dancing. The strict separation between what regular people do and what dancers can do is part of Robbins's choreographic thinking—part of his outlook that dancing matters for its craft and accomplishment as well as for its ability to represent societal dynamics and personal relationships. He put many kinds of walking on stage, especially in his comic works, such as the caricaturing entrances for the various characters in *The Concert.* The function of the walking, as for the entrance in *Dances* by the Boy in Brown, is to direct our attention to the dancing.

Edwin Denby—as one can see in the quotation excerpted above from his late essay—had a different perspective. He was fascinated by movement in general, both everyday movement on the street and trained movement in studios and theaters, and he attended to both with respect and humor. More, he was fascinated by perception itself. And his imagination was huge.

Shortly after NYCB gave the world premiere of *Dances at a Gathering,* in 1969, Denby interviewed Robbins about the work for *Dance Magazine.* Although Robbins later wrote a letter to the magazine, protesting how Denby had seen certain passages, the difference between the way each man spoke of his reflections in the interview itself gives a remarkable sense of how each saw theatrical dance. Robbins cannot help classifying; his thought is hardwired to do that, and the effect is distancing, yet also clarifying and intellectual. Here is part of his explanation to Denby of how he arrived at the conclusion of *Dances,* where the cast splits into couples, each man taking a woman's arm while they saunter around the stage, as the lighting shades into the dying day:

> The end of it had to come out of the scherzo, that very restless piece which ends with them all sort of *whoosh* running out—disappearing like cinders falling out into the night, and it couldn't end there, either. That's not the end of it, that's not how I feel about these people—that they went *whoosh* and disappeared. They are still here and they still move like dancers. They take . . . "a *passeggiata*"—they take a stroll, like in an Italian town, around the town's square at sundown [Nocturne]. They may have felt a threat, but they don't panic, they stay.
>
> . . .
>
> So coming back after the scherzo to the stage and the floor that we dance on, and putting your hand on it—if it's the earth or a ballet dancer's relationship to a wood floor—*that* somehow is the ending I knew I had to get to somewhere.

By 1969, Denby had not been reviewing dance regularly for several decades. He never published a review of *Dances at a Gathering;* his wonderful reflections on it were mentioned in passing in the context of his *Dance Magazine* interview with Robbins. They were not included in the posthumous collected *Dance Writings;* one finds them in the magazine itself and excerpts of them in Nancy Reynolds's indispensable *Repertory in Review: 40 Years of the New York City Ballet* from 1977. Altogether, they are no longer than a couple of paragraphs—but what marvels those are, especially for readers who have seen the ballet. Denby goes beyond reporting, beyond analysis, beyond evaluation. He doesn't showcase how much he knows or how hard he has looked and listened. He lives inside the action as if it were reality and he was writing its memoir. Here, suitable for a ten-year-old to appreciate, is his account of *Dance*'s opening moments:

> The curtain goes up in silence on an empty stage. It looks enormous. The back is all sky—some kind of changeable late afternoon in summer. Both sides of the stage are black. Forestage right, a man enters slowly, deep in thought. He is wearing a loose white shirt, brown tights, and boots. He turns to the sky and walks slowly away from you to center stage. You think of a man alone in a meadow. As he walks you notice the odd tilt of his head— like a man listening, inside himself. In the silence the piano begins as if he were remembering the music. He marks a dance step, he sketches a mazurka gesture, with a kind of pensive vigor he begins to improvise and now he is dancing marvelously and, in a burst of freedom he is running all over the meadow. Suddenly he subsides and, more mysterious than ever, slides into the woods and is gone.

Robbins himself would never have written anything like this. It is about something other than dancing that happens to be tendered *by* dancing to the writer. The dance matters precisely because it is not the subject.

3 steps

For individuals who dance be-cause they want to—amateurs or professionals, growing up or growing old, healthy or seeking to regain health in body or mind—the answer to the ques-tion, "Why does dance matter?" is as personal and self-evident as the answer to the question, "Why does breathing matter?": it mat-ters to the universe because it matters to you. A dancer who wants to be dancing is impelled through time and space from within, in a codified movement language or one that the dancer improvises, to exemplify or re-spond to rhythm that may be internally or externally generated.

Most of us, at some point in our lives, will dance—or at least move some part of our person in rhythm to a musical beat—irresistibly, because we're wired so that music moves us, even when we're tone deaf, and we can't help trying to keep time with it, even those of us who lack any mastery of rhythm. Many of us will also have had the experience of dancing deliberately, often in a ritual or social context, such as at a wedding or prom or rave or school performance or prayer service, to fit in or to be part of a community. And a few of us, usually self-selected, will have devoted a part of our life to dancing as a blindly chosen, one might even say sacred, calling. Not all devotees become dancers; some were (or still are) dance aficionados only. But a great many can be identified by their experience of an epiphany concerning dance in performance. For Anna Pavlova it was attending a matinee of the czar's Imperial Ballet in *The Sleeping Beauty*. For Frederick Ashton it was seeing a program by Isadora Duncan. For George Balanchine it was peering through a keyhole at the school of the Imperial Theater and witnessing three aspiring ballerinas. For Alvin Ailey it was seeing a program by Katherine Dunham and her company, especially her strong cohort of male dancers. For the critic and editor Robert Gottlieb it was attending Balanchine's brand-new *Orpheus* as a high school student.

Whatever leads you to take the first step into dance, on either side of the footlights, the usual (and essential) provocation to keep on with it is the continual possibility that in the course of dancing you will experience a state of creative flow—an ephemeral condition that unites thinking and action, as if one were sailing or flying or were otherwise motivated by an outside force to keep going without assistance. Ballerinas—for example, Vera

Zorina—have written about this condition. The flow is not in the movements themselves. And it is not independently visible. It is a catalyst that makes the movements legible to anyone watching you dance. When teachers and choreographers refer to dancing as what takes place *between* the steps, they are referring to this unifying, and clarifying, connectivity.

However, the question "Why does *looking* at dance matter?" is not so quickly addressed. Gottlieb has noted that as some people are tone deaf, others are dance deaf. Just as I can't whistle, they can't find dancing of interest or value. Is the reason physiological, like color blindness? Or is there any ultimate reason? Sometimes, those who disparage dance don't find the human body moving around in patterns worth watching unless the whole process is tied to a competition score. Sometimes, they think that dancing ruins the experience of music. Sometimes, they believe that dancing is a part of childhood one is meant to outgrow, like baby teeth. Now and then, they shun dancing—and its historic link to beauty—as intellectually wayward or as downright wicked. Most often, though, in my experience, they dismiss dance as too difficult to understand. They just don't get it, the way some readers don't take to poetry because of the testable "hidden meanings" on whose existence they explain their high school English teacher had insisted.

From time to time, though, even I try to whistle, vain as the attempts are; and now and then even the adversaries of dance get curious about what they disdain or dismiss. Why is it so tough to understand? they ask, meaning, Why does it bore me when opera (or live theater, or cabaret, or painting) doesn't? After many years of trying to argue with them, I've arrived at a point where I agree that they're on to something: in certain respects, dance is indeed hard to understand. If you consider dancing seriously—as something more worthy of your concentration than gazing at a Lava Lite—then you quickly learn that even for a short, simple number there is quite a lot of information to take in, and to do so requires fast eyes, keen hearing, and a capacious memory. There are elements in any dance, regardless of the tradition or style, that are difficult simply to recognize as they go by, much less analyze and then discuss, just as there are indeed layers of possible significance to poetry that begin to reveal themselves only after many rereadings. Of course, for the purpose of discussion, it helps to have a basic vocabulary of steps, poetic meters, musical forms—something that will assist you to identify rhythms, how the art behaves in time. Yet that vocabulary is not relevant to your emotional response, and it is not necessary to figuring out reasons for why you respond as you do.

For whatever complexity or secret you may discover for yourself in a work of art, it is rarely placed there by the maker intentionally as a coded message, much less a prank (too tough to do, and why bother?); and even if—in order to bypass censorship—the artist has implanted a code, your appreciation and enjoyment of the whole is almost never affected by its resolution through critical analysis. Nor are an audience member's intuitions of a "secret" statement in a work "merely" fantasies, subjectively generated by the audience and imposed on the works at will, like daydreams. Rather, these associations among a work's elements, which gradually reveal themselves as you deepen acquaintance with the whole, are collaborative constructions between it and you. On occasion, as the photographer Robert Doisneau has recommended for photographers, the choreographer or author may have built in the ingredients for associations along with prompts guiding the audience or reader to complete them—although if they are left uncompleted it doesn't matter to one's engagement with the image. Association is an added enrichment, as at the end of Ashton's ballet of young lovers, *The Two Pigeons* (1960), when some in the audience can't help tearing up, at every performance, upon seeing the second in a pair of live doves swoop onto the stage to join the lonely first, as if from a long sojourn away. This special effect wouldn't be special, though, if the sense it prompts of harmony restored hadn't been prepared for by the choreography for human beings that came before it and if it weren't also underwritten by the tenderness of the André Messager score at that point. If you were just to see one dove on stage and another fly out from the wings to join it, absent the rest of the ballet, it would be arresting, like a magic trick, but it wouldn't bring tears.

Simply trying to appreciate what actually takes place in a dance—the facts of dance action—is hard enough. A more extreme brain workout is trying to witness what the dancers are doing while remaining aware of the theatrical effects or illusions their movement is intended for the audience to see. If the choreography is coordinated to a musical score, then to recognize and track points of coordination as they happen and be able to recall them later should earn you admission to Mensa. And trying to keep track of all this while remaining receptive to whatever epiphanies of meaning the dance may provoke—and perhaps while being overtaken by rapture, too—requires a type of multitasking in which your consciousness, so to speak, has one eye on the stage and one watching your brain be a brain. I can understand why those to whom such complication is the last thing desired at the end of a day would long to take a walk, perhaps in search of the nearest Lava Lite—or Bud Lite. That is why, thinking of them, I extend the invitation in this chapter to take a walk with me among dances where the multitasking might prove not only as useful to brain health as sudoku but even more enjoyable.

Among the major themes running through this peregrination is that of unscripted memory. Like music, dancing attracts prodigies of memory among its performers (though not among as many of its creators) and among its chroniclers, such as the critics Deborah Jowitt, who has a singular memory for movement, and Alastair Macaulay, whose recollection of particular choreographic passages and of timelines in dance history rarely fails to astonish. You might think that dancers, with their core-deep muscle memories, would make the preservation of a dance business as usual. Well, "as usual" meaning if the dancers work very carefully to pass the dance from one generation to another and to keep it fresh and important, like an icon or the Torah. Some dances are preserved that way. In terms of Western concert works, the oldest known ballet to have retained its more-or-less unchanged original choreography (the pointe work for the women confounds belief) is the comedy *The Whims of Cupid and the Ballet Master,* preserved by the Royal Danish Ballet, for which it was made by Vincenzo Galeotti (1733–1816), the company's founder, in 1786. The story is "meet cute" with a twist: ten pairs of lovers are blindfolded by Cupid and then partners are switched. I saw the Danes perform this during the Bournonville Festival, in Copenhagen, in 1979; storytelling and pantomime were in the foreground, with some dance. In the United States, Philadelphian John Durang's Sailor's Hornpipe, which Durang performed with the Lewis Hallam troupe in the late 1700s, is still performable, because Durang's son, also a dancer, valued it and took care to write down the steps.

Most astonishing, at least to me, is when not only the text of a dance is preserved but also the emotion of it. Take *Awassa Astrige/Ostrich,* the spellbinding solo dance created in 1932 by the native musician and choreographer of Sierra Leone Asadata Dafora (born John Warner Dafora Horton, 1890–1965), celebrated as the inventor of dance-dramas showcasing West African dances and tales, a collaborator as well with Orson Welles and John Houseman. There is no film I know of with Dafora in his ostrich solo, but there are other films of him in solos from the same period of composition. Films are available of his student, the choreographer and erstwhile Katherine Dunham dancer Charles Moore, a performer of regal fidelity to dance style and personal warmth, as the ostrich (I saw Moore perform the dance, taught to him by Dafora, on stage in the 1970s). And films can be seen of the solo as rendered by younger dancers from the Alvin Ailey American Dance Company (where Dafora's dance is still in repertory), the Dallas Black Dance Theater, and the Dayton Contemporary Dance Company (whose filmed performance from the late 1990s by G. D. Harris is outstanding). *Awassa Astrige* is a proud walking dance-parade in a half circle for a tall male dancer with a beautiful body who offers a special strength in the shoulders and back. The steps are deliberative, with a strong demi-plié that evokes the sprinter's limbs of the bird; the power of the upper spine from which the arms wing out is constantly emphasized with a rippling motion. (I wouldn't be surprised to learn that Dafora, a cosmopolitan artist, had seen Anna Pavlova's swan solo, live or on film.) Midway, the soloist pauses center stage and takes a fully turned-out grand plié facing the audience, and his body turns into an abstract double-chevron design, similar to those of the bent-kneed figures one finds on nineteenth-century West African sculptures and dance masks. It is a bold, stunning moment, framed by a walk so well translated from that of the animal to which this dance is in homage that the dancer seems mysteriously to embody the spirit of the creature. *Awassa Astrige,* ninety years old, its checkable revivals captured on film, calls into question the received idea that dance is exclusively an art form of vanishing works.

On the other hand, I've witnessed more than a few rehearsals when even fellow members of an original cast will disagree about what they did in performance and what they understood the choreographer to want from their dancing in the process of making the work. An example from the year 2000 springs to mind. Twice weekly, over that entire year, I participated as a co-interviewer, with Monica Moseley, in an extensively detailed oral history of the beloved ballet star Frederic Franklin, a collaboration between the Jerome Robbins Dance Division of the New York Public Library for the Performing Arts and the George Balanchine Foundation, of which, today, only the audio tapes, I, and the transcripts remain. As part of the oral history on Franklin's years in the mid-1940s with the Ballet Russe de Monte Carlo, when he served Balanchine as a rehearsal master and assistant, I also conducted an interview by phone with the surrealist painter and poet Dorothea Tanning, the original designer of *The Night Shadow* (soon after the premiere the definite article was dropped), Balanchine's unsettling 1946 melodrama for the Ballet Russe. (Balanchine revived it, in 1960, as *La Sonnambula* for Allegra Kent at the New York City Ballet.) Tanning, then a mere lass of ninety (she died in 2012, at one hundred and one), was actively publishing poems in the *New Yorker* and demonstrated a crackerjack command of her past. Meanwhile, Franklin, then a mere lad of eighty-six (he died in 2013, at the age of ninety-nine), was demonstrating his famed powers of eidetic memory twice a week at the library—identifying hordes of dancers in uncaptioned photographs, describing elements of choreography that had been dropped in silent performance films from the 1940s of ballets that were never again revived, and performing other kinds of memory bravura.

The Franklin and Tanning interviews concerning *The Night Shadow* were delightfully complementary—up until their conflicting views on the final lighting cue. Tanning insisted that she and Balanchine had decided on a mystical effect at the end: the image of the light from the Sleepwalker's candle—which the audience is asked to imagine she is able to hold reliably while also carrying the collapsed body of the murdered Poet in her arms as she proceeds up an interior staircase and then along a second-floor corridor—would flash from window to window as she "passed by," and then, in an understated transition against the laws of

Nature but following the pressure of art, the candle's light alone would continue out the last window to float into the night sky. (Late in the last century, for a performance or two, American Ballet Theatre deployed that effect in its production of *La Sonnambula*. An emotion of awe, prepared for by Balanchine's haunted dances and the inevitable violence of the story line, in conjunction with Vittorio Rieti's plaintive arrangement of one of Bellini's arias, left some observers deeply moved, me among them.) But Franklin, on whom Balanchine had constructed the role of the Poet and who served Balanchine at the Ballet Russe as rehearsal master for the choreographer's repertory there, was adamant that the light never left the Baron's mansion, not even once experimentally. That final effect of the candlelight—trapped? liberated?—does not change the uneasy tone or peculiar temperament of the ballet, whose events are strange enough, but the choice of ending does affect the way one may think about its meaning.

Tanning and Franklin offered viable yet contradictory meanings. But these gothic ambiguities, for reasons I can't articulate yet strongly feel, seem in keeping with what *The Night Shadow* was fundamentally about. One possible resolution: Tanning's surrealist designs for the ballet were not retained long enough to make an impression even on Franklin, the original Poet. Tanning designed the set as a yellow-green wax world that seemed to be melting from within—as if the action took place inside the Sleepwalker's candle—and she also designed such headpieces for the women attending the Baron's party as a huge clock and the model of a sailing ship, evocative of the elaborate pouf wigs of Louis XVI's court. Tanning's designs lasted only for the ballet's first season, however, to be replaced by a set and costumes by someone else that were much more conventional. *The Night Shadow* did not play well on the Ballet Russe's cross-country tour: it was too strange. In context, it makes sense that a puzzling production effect, such as Tanning's liberation of the candlelight into the night sky, would be scaled back along with the rest of her designs.

Given the energy of this disagreement over one lighting cue between just two former collaborators, you might expect that six individuals gathering to wrangle back from muscle memory an entire dance—last performed decades ago and never previously filmed—would offer up some raucous hours. Archival videos of one such group in such an attempt show that you'd be correct.

In the late 1980s, Martha Graham oversaw, in addition to her main company, the founding of a smaller performing group for younger dancers, called the Martha Graham Dance Ensemble. Yuriko Kikuchi—the Graham star "Yuriko"—then director of the ensemble, took on the task of reconstructing Graham's *Celebration* (1934), a dance for twelve women of some four hundred jumps and considerable communal intensity (as Barbara Morgan's photographs of the original airborne dancers show) to a score for drum and trumpet by Louis Horst.

Yuriko recounts the process of working with five members of the original cast in her and Emiko Tokunaga's biography-autobiography, *Yuriko: An American Japanese Dancer: To Wash in the Rain and Polish with the Wind* (2008). She began her reconstructive work alone, starting from films made by Graham dancer Jane Dudley in a much earlier (unsuccessful) effort to reconstruct the dance. Then, after two weeks, Yuriko initiated reconstructive rehearsals with the veteran originals. "Of course, there were many disagreements among the original cast," Yuriko noted, and a reader can hear the unstated weariness in that "of course." Fortunately, she filmed those rehearsals, and her films make it clear why, after two weeks of many rehearsal hours a day, she—herself an award-winning choreographer who directed her own company for a decade—dismissed her colleagues and shaped the final section herself in order to have something in time to teach to the ensemble. (The main company could not perform the reconstruction, Yuriko explains, because "there were too many jumps." Jumping like that is for the young.) "We showed it to Martha, who was pleased, and it was well received by the audience," Yuriko adds.

I can attest to the audience's thrilled enthusiasm, not only for this reconstruction by Yuriko of an early Graham work for the young dancers of the ensemble, but for all her ensemble reconstructions. During the 1980s, Yuriko embarked on a project to bring back long-unseen masterpieces from Graham's first, all-women group of the 1930s. These works feature Graham's early version of her technique, which emphasized mass; jumps that seemed to pop up from nowhere; epic contractions that would be 6 or above on the Richter scale, were they geological events across the land rather than actions confined in the living human torso; and falls to the front and back, where the body looked like an Easter Island sculpture toppling. I learned much about that early Graham technique from Ethel Butler, another original member of Graham's first company, who was invited by former Graham dancer Paul Taylor to give classes in it at his school. (When men began to join the Graham company, beginning with ballet-trained Erick Hawkins in the late 1930s, Graham's technique acquired more spiraling movement around the back and more nuance in all aspects, thereby enhancing male-female partnering and erasing some of its early staunch modernist-feminist impersonality.)

As Yuriko recounts in Tokunaga's book, one day in the 1980s she happened to be in the company archives, and she saw that films existed of the older dances, which inspired her to reconstruct them. "What came to my mind was that it was like going to a cemetery, digging up a coffin, and resurrecting a person/dance—that had been buried for a long, long time. If I could bring it alive—the past—I wondered if it would be accepted now. That was my curiosity. You see, I always start with questions. Is it possible? Will it be possible? Can I do it?" She began with *Heretic,* from 1929, which enjoys a film that is complete and features Graham herself dancing the central persecuted victim. Graham, who was skeptical that Yuriko could bring back the dance in a viable form, did not participate at all in the process, except to give Yuriko permission to proceed.

But before any work could begin in the studio, with living dancers, Yuriko found that for her to preserve the life of the work in a cultural and societal context sixty years forward from the one in which it was made, she had to undergo a transformation in her view of it. To justify bringing *Heretic* back from the grave, her reconstruction had to be a contemporary reinterpretation as well.

I saw especially that the group work had tremendous intensity—with Martha in a white gown and the others in black. It was like she was trapped—I put it into a dramatic conte[x]t, like a Black person caught in the White community surrounded with hate, or it could be a person caught in a community/high school bullied and picked upon by the majority and not wanting to become one of them. In looking back now, I suppose that being Japanese American, being evacuated and hated, this may have come to my mind with the realization that the Blacks were the most discriminated people in America.

I used the Ensemble to recreate this dance, but I had to bring it to my understanding of immediacy—now. That is why I selected the black/white issue as a theme. As the whole group was formed into a semi-circle or v-shape diagonal, and the music was so barren (which was Louis Horst's composition based on an Old Breton Song) that what came to mind was a tall building diagonally towering over the victim, which was the power I wanted to create.

What I could have done was just to copy the film, but it did not apply to now, and the 1987 audience would remain untouched. I felt that just copying the steps and performing the formations did not communicate the meaning and value of the piece. The interpretation of Martha's part was her desperation to resist being pulled into the group sentiments. Within any group of people, there is a solitary figure that does not want to belong to the majority—Martha frequently portrayed this solitary figure alone and apart from everyone, like in *Primitive Mysteries*.

I finished it and MGE [the dancers of the Martha Graham Ensemble] showed it to Martha in the studio. She was shocked. Martha and everyone who saw it liked it so much, they shifted the whole dance on to the company.

During seven decades of devoted artistry to Graham—including as a performer, a teacher, and a stager of Graham's works for the company, the ensemble, dance companies internationally, and many schools throughout the United States—Yuriko put some ten of the early dances on their feet as either reconsidered revivals or full reconstructions. A group of those dances featured passages of walking crafted like ancient prayers; to me, they suggest that the dances containing them could be considered demonstrations of Graham's reverence for her practice of dance as an art. These core "walking" works include "Steps in the Street" from *Chronicle, El Penitente,* and, most prominently, *Primitive Mysteries.* In all these, the cast enters the stage by a ritual walk, unique to each dance. Most dramatic is the backward walking entrance, in silence, of "Steps in the Street" for twelve women, the body of each dancer slightly torquing to face her upraised left hand, which the dancer regards with sadness and pain, as if the hand belonged to someone suffering more. Each backward step is taken first with the arch of one foot, and then, in a separate movement, the heel is lowered and weight shifted, as if the feet had been broken but the person forced to go on. So, in the later passage when the ensemble reenters to music, using that analyzed walk but facing forward and in double time, the transformation prepares the cast and the audience for the incendiary jumps to come. "Steps in the Street" is often associated with Pablo Picasso's tormented and enraged painting *Guernica* as a representation of Graham's response to the atrocities of the Spanish Civil War. In addition, placed in the third "Dances After Catastrophe" section of *Chronicle,* "Steps" carries a subhead of "Devastation—Homelessness—Exile," which also links it to the Stateside miseries of the Great Depression. The dance contributes a bitter twist to that Zimbabwean adage, accenting the "if" in "If you can walk, you can dance."

In 1964, as a tribute to Louis Horst, Graham revived for her company three works for which Horst had written the score. Among them was her masterpiece of 1931, *Primitive Mysteries,* a pristine example of sophisticated modernist dance architecture married to an image of a rural village celebration for the Virgin Mary, who also, in her action, evokes some of Christ's miracles and Crucifixion, all set to Horst's delicate score for flute and drum. (Horst composed the music after the dance itself was fully made and presented to him in silence. He thought the silence effective for the walking entrances to each of the three sections, and Graham retained it.) Originally, the work was cast for twelve women (in subsequent productions the number has been increased) wearing long, exactingly simple deep-blue dresses, with Graham at their center in a cloud of overlapping white organdy panels, a garment appropriate for something between a wedding and an infant's baptism.

In that production of 1964, Yuriko took Graham's central role. A film of her performance exists: magically, her dancing is both girlishly light in its impulse—the painstaking walks of the group become, on Yuriko, airily upswinging high legs and high arches—and metaphorically heavy, that is, powerful, thanks to the spatial expanse her limbs and her costume occupy. I've seen other dancers on stage in this part—Janet Eilber (the current director of the Graham Company), Yuriko Kimura, Takako Asakawa—and they were very fine; even so, none achieved that paradoxical quality one sees in Yuriko on the film from 1964. Nevertheless, *Primitive Mysteries* remains breathtaking to anyone being introduced to it. As the esteemed critic Nancy Goldner wrote of a later revival by Sophie Maslow, in 1977, for the Graham Company—the most encompassing and brilliantly written appreciation of this dance I know, published in the *Nation* of June 4, 1977—"Its integrity is such that almost any Virgin could convince us of her symbolic power, simply by virtue of her dance's design."

Choreographers of stature tend to take great care in how their dancers walk in their works; still, few have taken as much care as Graham in getting the walking in *Primitive Mysteries* how she wanted it. In the memoir *Bird's Eye View* (2002), Dorothy Bird— one of the members of the original production of 1934—writes about the arduous search that Graham and her company embarked on to create the walk.

> The walk was to be the seed of the style. In quiet, unpressured rehearsals with her group, Martha meticulously analyzed the coordination of the body as she searched for the precise dramatic quality that would best communicate to the audience exactly what she had in mind. Her patience was inexhaustible. During countless hours of rehearsal, over a period of months, we walked side by side in groups of three or four, without holding hands but with the knuckles of our cupped hands pressed lightly against the knuckles of the person next to us. Once she placed a broom handle across the backs of our shoulders to hold them flat as we walked in groups of three as a unit. Martha decreed that no one should lead, and no one should follow. With no word cues or sounds of any kind, we progressed from walking to an easy loping run, which developed into a wild, free run, similar to the run of untamed horses, hair flying, like the hair of women running in a painting by Picasso.

Then, without an outside cue of any kind, we slowed down, changing smoothly to a walk that gradually became slower and slower
until we were almost not moving at all, and finally, gradually, we
came to a stop. It was exciting to be absolutely still after the wild
run, and to be a part of the trio that moved as one.

Bird adds that the dancers would go to Coney Island and walk
against the waves of the Atlantic Ocean in order to practice the
quality of resistance against a natural force that Graham wanted.

What makes this exploration in the studio remarkable (apart
from the extraordinary amount of time spent on discovering and
perfecting a single kind of movement) is the goal that the ensemble should ambulate together as a cohesive organism essentially
by breathing as one, without physical or verbal cues, motivated
by a sense of community that took months to develop. To compare an arena-sized example of such community: on YouTube
you can see a spectacular synchronized routine for forty women
in white suits and blue neckerchiefs in a precision walking competition, during which the competitors go through scores of complex transformations, at one point moonwalking in sync; however, to achieve their effects, they have a leader screaming out
commands. The silences of the Graham work in conjunction
with the astonishing, leaderless communion of the group are, for
me, important to what makes *Primitive Mysteries* a great work of
art and the precision walking competitors outstanding exemplars
of a sport. There are collectively practiced rituals in Catholic
Spain whose effects are partially similar to Graham's: As the doc-
umentarian Brandon Li has filmed in Andalucía, the annual Passion ceremony called Tronos de Semana Santa (Thrones of Holy

Week) involves scores of men who belong to local religious broth-erhoods. Locked into lines under massive religious sculptures, the men shoulder long rods to hoist aloft and walk through the streets the relevant throne for twelve hours at a time; each throne weighs up to eleven thousand pounds. A glancing shot of the oxford-shod feet of the throne-bearers shows them to be mov-ing under that crushing burden in exact synchrony. In *Primitive Mysteries,* a secular construction, the terrible weight of suffering and responsibility is evoked, even though the actual cause is nei-ther visible nor literal. All that practicing in the ocean back in 1931 continues to be of use today.

In the fall of 2007, for a project sponsored by the Dance No-tation Bureau, Yuriko was flown to Southern Methodist Univer-sity in Dallas, Texas, to stage *Primitive Mysteries* on the under-graduates. For a panel on the work and on Yuriko's stagings, the dance critic Clive Barnes, his wife, Valerie, and I were flown down to Dallas as well. The students were very excited and clearly en-joyed their time with Yuriko. Alas, that weekend, Yuriko injured her back and, in pain and distress, had to fly home to New York a full day earlier than she'd planned. Returned to the city, she learned that she needed surgery. I visited her several times while she took physical therapy at the hospital and taught herself to walk again at home. She had to analyze the mechanics of walk-ing on her own body. In watching her teach herself what walking is—what the joints do, what the weight-bearing muscles do, how to place the spine, how to take each step by carefully placing the foot and rolling through it from arch to flat, most especially how to bear up under discomfort and soldier on—I gained a tremendous appreciation for the freedom of being able to walk down the street and for the treasure a dancer's decades of discipline can prove when discipline and morale are needed in daily life.

I also was inspired to read about walking: about the importance of memory and imagination in locating us to ourselves in relation to the optic flow of the world passing by, or about the vestibular system of the inner ear, which controls the balance of mammals with a spine—what Shane O'Mara, professor of experimental brain research at Trinity College Dublin, calls, in his book *In Praise of Walking* (2019), "a miracle of micro-engineering." So much of walking turns out to take place in the head! Can dancing be far behind? One day, I thought, perhaps I'll be able to acknowledge Yuriko's long and arduous retutoring of her body to move on its own as my inspiration for becoming curious about how our imagination of what we might do affects our story of what we have done and our consciousness of what we are doing.

Yuriko Kikuchi, born in 1920, died in 2022, a little over a month after she celebrated her one hundred and second birthday.

4 floatings

Wire walking: It's the most difficult art in the world and the easiest art in the world. It's the art of walking—except they don't teach that in universities. People do that naturally. [Wire walking] has to be a very mysterious and very personal chemistry that you develop by intuition, by passion, and by practicing all the time.

—PHILIPPE PETIT, REFLECTING ON HIS HIGH-WIRE WALK BETWEEN THE TWIN TOWERS, SOME THIRTEEN HUNDRED FEET ABOVE THE STREET, ON AUGUST 7, 1974

Era: late eighteenth-century Edo period in Japan, in the city of Edo (later called Tokyo), a moment when its burgeoning population of nearly a million souls was going to make it the most populous city in the world and when Utamaro, the master of ukiyo-e woodblock printing that flourished there, was translating his visual perceptions of sex workers in the brothels into breathtaking visions of female beauty. Place: an upscale teahouse, where a new courtesan, her face whitened with rice powder, her lips rouged to a Heian court pout, is about to be presented to a patron. Wearing geta sandals whose lacquered soles elevate her half a foot above the ground, she is walking along a wooden floor in a sort of parade, called, in English, a "promenade." She takes one step, then, balancing her weight on that leg, she takes a second, rather different kind of step: she drags that second foot along the floor in a scooping motion, as if her foot was attached to a ball and chain—which, metaphorically, it is.

Of course, we are not, in fact, inside an actual Edo period brothel. We are inside a movie: the film *Sharaku* (1995), directed by Masahiro Shinoda, about a historical ukiyo-e artist nicknamed Sharaku (Impertinent), a contemporary of Utamaro's, who emerges into historical records from nowhere and, over two years in the 1790s, produces some 140 woodblock portraits of Kabuki actors, then, as suddenly, disappears. In contrast to Utamaro, celebrated for his art in his own time, Sharaku's art was considered pedestrian; his portraits only came to be treasured long after there was any trace of his existence in the chronicles.

A little more might be said about this moment in the picture. Film buffs and cineastes may see a bow to earlier masters of Jap-

anese cinema. Could there be a fleeting identification on director Shinoda's part with Sharaku himself? There is a gently floated
analogy between the graded relationships of craftsmanship and
prestige that link Sharaku with Utamaro, on the one hand, and,
on the other, use *Sharaku* to invoke the classic, fictionalized bi-
opic *Utamaro and His Five Women* (1946), by the revered filmmaker Kenji Mizoguchi, where one finds an entire brothel of
courtesans, each with her right arm poised on the left arm of her
patron, taking a ceremonial promenade through the center of
town, courtesan after courtesan dragging her scooped foot to
meet the stalwart standing leg: through the magic of the movies,
the ritual image of repression becomes converted into a visually
delightful corps de ballet. (Surely the origin of the idiosyncratic
gait is that the elevation of the women's shoes make that scooping the only way for the wearer to walk with any degree of grace,
rather than having to awkwardly lift up the foot and clomp down
with every step.) Film critics and historians have suggested that
Mizoguchi was using the figure of Utamaro as a lens for his own
autobiography, which the filmmaker was smuggling in disguised
as history, owing to constrictions on public statements in effect
during the years when the United States occupied Japan. By including one step of the *Utamaro* promenade by one courtesan in
Sharaku, Shinoda suggests that he, too, is slipping in a bit of autobiography as a filmmaker relative to the older master.

In speculating about these meanings of a rather simple choreographic moment, I cannot tell you that Shinoda would be in
agreement with them or, if he would be, that they were intended
when the film was made. They are my conclusions (sometimes

shared by other writers, sometimes not) based on my observation and readings of related material. In literary or film or music criticism, such a caveat would be unnecessary; the distinction between textual scholarship and interpretation usually goes without saying, and in the event of a reader's uncertainty or disagreement, the original text (or some version of it) is available to consult. In the case of movement as an art, though, despite the wide use of film, the personal recollections of previous casts, and the occasional practice of notation, the very notion of a text remains in question. Yet, even when the term may not indicate, or be understood to mean, anything more definite than a floating world of stage directions, performance options, and historical precedents, it does point to a consensus on the matter of whether Dance-X falls into the category of "I'll know it when I see it."

Although physical logic, usually through step-by-step analysis, is crucial to making any dance comprehensible to its practitioners as they learn to do it or as they participate in its creation, in order to make daytime sense to an audience a dance must somehow also, on some level, *illogically* connect, instantaneously and mysteriously. Absent that connection, dancing as an art matters only to those to whom it already matters. It continues to amaze me that a few individual dancers, such as Anna Pavlova or Margot Fonteyn or Michael Jackson, effect that immediate connection worldwide, inspiring appreciation among millions of individuals who could never communicate with one another through verbal language and who would be unlikely to enjoy their neighbors' native music or dance traditions but who all immediately understand the dancer. This was especially the case with Pavlova, who spread her version of ballet as easily as Johnny Appleseed casting his seeds. Pavlova made ballet a global lingua franca—throughout the United States and Europe, in India, Japan, and elsewhere in Asia, and in Latin America. How on earth could so many people who had so little in common all be ready and willing to rejoice in such a specific theatrical practice for which Pavlova was a self-appointed missionary? The question could also be posed concerning the RKO films of Fred Astaire and Ginger Rogers, beloved worldwide since they were first released in the 1930s. If the answer were perfection of dance technique, or American imperialism in cultural matters, then Pavlova would be knocked into the corner pocket. If the answer were depth of Russian soul, then Astaire and Rogers would be sidelined. Whatever makes a star who appeals worldwide and for generations, it is not only a matter of excellence in what the performers and their presenters can more or less control. It is in part a matter of what they cannot.

For years, Fred Astaire had the idea that he could somehow, through the magic of Hollywood, dance on a ceiling. Possibly his thought went back to 1934, the release year for the Gaumont-British musical film *Evergreen,* where Jessie Matthews, the British star of musical comedy (dubbed the feminine counterpart of Fred Astaire and the optimal partner for him by the *New York Times*), sang and then, in the art deco ballet choreography of Buddy Bradley, kicked her long-stemmed legs to her temples, poured herself into rococo backbends, and navigated a flawless manège of regulation chaîné turns to the heaven-sent Rodgers and Hart song "Dancing on the Ceiling." Astaire apparently wanted to work with Matthews, and she was considered for the part that Joan Fontaine, a nineteen-year-old non-dancer, ultimately was given in Astaire's *Damsel in Distress* (1937), an RKO picture, set in London, for which Astaire requested that his co-star be someone other than Rogers. (He wanted more RKO films without her but got at least that one.) Astaire and Matthews never connected on screen; however, Astaire did finally get to dance on the ceiling—by himself—in the MGM musical *Royal Wedding* (1951) to a new song, "You're All the World to Me" (music by Burton Lane, lyrics by Alan Jay Lerner). The emotional image is also different: instead of love transforming the Matthews character so that a dance performed in a windowless apartment feels to her, and to her audience, as if she is floating on clouds, the Astaire character—who, in the story, cannot speak of his affections—dances inside a revolving world, an evocation of his close-held feelings.

Dance-film scholar John Mueller (*Astaire Dancing: The Musical Films,* 1985) confirmed in an interview with Astaire that Astaire took responsibility for all the choreography he himself performed in his films, including those where he worked out duets with Hermes Pan. The solution to how he achieved the trick of this particular number—seeming to dance 360 degrees around a furnished room while keeping the bib of his formal wear starched and every hair in place—was not the director's (Stanley Donen) or the associate choreographer's (Nick Castle). It came to Astaire one morning at 4:00 a.m.: build the room as a rotating cube (the crew called it the squirrel cage), bolt down all the furniture, props, and the camera, and somehow rotate the camera operator as well, so that, when Astaire was literally dancing on the ceiling, the cameraman and the camera were upside-down. Mueller notes that of all Astaire's numbers in his thirty-one musical pictures, this is probably his most famous—and that its actual choreography in terms of Astaire's dancing is comparatively mundane. (I protest about the middle section, where Astaire's taps and hand slaps engage the orchestra with delightful rhythmic acuity.) What is not mundane, however, is the mission of the illusion—to seem to escape gravity, not as a metaphor but as an element of Newtonian physics, and to look as if it's easy-peasy to do. In fact, as with many attempts to make literal and simple something that everyday living does for us without our even trying, such as the feeling of taking a walk around one's room or of falling in love, the logistics, structural planning, and execution of "You're All the World to Me" were so intricate and laborious (and, I'm guessing, expensive) that Astaire, besieged by curious fans about it, used to carry around a diagram to show how the number was achieved.

I'm continuously surprised by how many of Astaire's dances are theme-and-variations developments of walking. For New Year of 2017, the Parisian film curator and editor N. T. Binh made a thirty-minute anthology on YouTube called "Dancing with Fred Astaire," and it is still posted there as I write. It contains treasures of pure dancing by Astaire with Rogers, Rita Hayworth, Eleanor Powell, Judy Garland, and Cyd Charisse and clips from other movies in which some of the embedded Astaire-Rogers numbers play an inspiring or wrenching emotional role in the story (*Pennies from Heaven, A Stranger Among Us, The English Patient, The Green Mile*). The theme of walking permeates the choreography. I was shocked to see a duet (perhaps the greatest of the Astaire-Rogers duets) I thought I knew like the back of my hand—"Let's Face the Music and Dance," from *Follow the Fleet*—that suddenly registered to my eye as 80 percent a walking dance. To witness *Top Hat*'s "Cheek to Cheek" in the company of *The Green Mile*'s death-row prisoner, who asks to see a movie as his final wish before the electric chair because he has never seen any movie—and watching what will be his one and only, he begins to weep as the feathers on Rogers's gown sinuously brush the air and the prisoner gently whispers "angels"—is to discover the number as if for the first time.

Astaire is not unique in cinema for making the act of walking seem both glamorous and universally accessible. One thinks, for instance, of John Travolta's charismatic gait in the "Staying Alive" number of *Saturday Night Fever* in 1977. Travolta's proud hustle down the sidewalk of Bay Ridge, Brooklyn, accompanied on the soundtrack by the Bee Gees, shares their pulse yet is not intimately engaged with other aspects of their music. He's too wrapped up in himself for engagement. John Badham's direction has arranged for their song to feel to us, watching, as if it's in the character's head the way a radio is in a car. It serves *him* as he strides, and from his perspective, its accents obey the accents of *his* steps as if he were the DJ for the street. This expressionist use of a soundtrack as an aural description of a character's subjective world goes back at least to Alfred Hitchcock's use of Bernard Herrmann's score to reveal the psychic workings of Norman Bates in *Psycho* (1960). A more immediate predecessor for Badham's generation was perhaps Stanley Kubrick's *A Clockwork Orange,* with its destructively sardonic matching of rape and murder as choreography from the perspectives of the perpetrators, thanks to the accompaniment of the recording of Gene Kelly singing the title song from the movie musical *Singin' in the Rain* (1952), the number that, more than any other in commercial movies, elevates the mood of an audience by linking love, childhood mischief (jumping in street puddles), and momentary defiance of nature (dancing in a rainstorm). At the time *A Clockwork Orange* was released in 1971, Kubrick's twists on Hollywood happiness into perversity and mayhem were taken by older audiences, who had long ago given their hearts to Gene Kelly's number in earnest, as something just short of desecration and by younger, draft-age audiences as an accurate reflection of the damage America was wreaking on Southeast Asia during the Vietnam War.

By 1977, however, the war was over, the draft had ended, and America was deeply invested in entertainment. This was the era of another "dance boom," in clubs via disco, in theaters large and small via the Regional Touring Program of the National Endowment for the Arts, and on television via *Dance in America* and *Live from Lincoln Center. Saturday Night Fever* was released the same year as Herbert Ross's popular ballet movie *The Turning Point,* written by Arthur Laurents, author of the script for *West Side Story.* That vintage year, 1977, also saw the premiere of *Vienna Waltzes,* Balanchine's hourlong extravaganza for NYCB, and the first spring season of American Ballet Theatre at the Metropolitan Opera House. In New York, at least, the decade of crime and graffiti notwithstanding, dance was back in a big way and with glamour. Yet *Saturday Night Fever,* which was not about glamour in fact but in dreams, caught the public imagination most intensely of all. The story is about a young man who, by luck, escaped the draft (which ended entirely in 1976) and who, unsure of what he is going to do with himself, pours his energies into self-taught club dancing, where one can exert some control over one's life and garner admiration of one's friends by dancing well. At the end of the movie, he begins to grow up, which, in his case, it is suggested, may mean shifting his priorities from dance to earning his own living, rather than relying on his parents. That his dancing may prove something entirely associated with the youth he will outgrow gives the picture a delicate touch of quintessentially American melancholy.

Some comic parental sidekicks are stationed throughout the RKO Astaire-Rogers pictures, but no parents; the dancers, already wised up about childhood's end, have to support themselves in the middle of the Great Depression. Astaire's dances for himself and his partners demonstrate how to negotiate the music that fate has dealt you with innovation and grace; in several of the duets, there are also bits of pure cinematic fantasy, where Astaire magicks Rogers out of her characteristic resistance to him and into his arms. The mission is to create pure pleasure through fine dancing, and when one only finds that blissful pleasure in the movies, one goes back to the movies often. In terms of rhythm (phrased or patterned pulse), scale of steps and gestures, constriction or ranginess in the way space is covered, the dancers maintain a steady dialogue with the shifting textures of the instrumental performances we hear—instrumental performances of the song Astaire has just sung (he never dances *to* anyone singing). As one can learn from Beth Genné's fascinating *Dance Me a Song: Astaire, Balanchine, Kelly, and the American Film Musical,* her study published in 2018 of leading movie choreographers, directors, and musical composers and arrangers in the 1930s and 1940s, even the loudness or softness of a score will be acknowledged by the choreography of an Astaire dance. Astaire's characters do not have a separate, subjective response to the music of dances other than the physical action of how they dance to it. What one sees is what they are, which is part of their enduring appeal. Furthermore, an additional subjective layer would be useless in a world where one doesn't have the option of going to college or enrolling in on-the-job training to improve one's station or class. You take what you get, make lemonade from lemons, and pray for the possibility of magic around the next corner. Without real options, you settle back and admire how simple happiness can be: the goes-without-saying simultaneity of sight and sound, as if dancers were just making up the dance while we watch them— as if we, ourselves, could pull up our morale by its proverbial bootstraps and change our own lives like that!

Of course, as Mueller, the critic Arlene Croce, Astaire himself, and his various collaborators have noted, how exhausting it is to get this simple effect onto the silver screen—as exhausting as it is to manufacture happiness for oneself on leaving the movie theater. The nature of the dance perfectionism that has been sweeping away audiences for nearly nine decades isn't what we encounter in the precision kickline of the Rockettes or in ballet companies where the corps consists of dancers who function as exactingly interchangeable units. When Astaire made a dance for himself, solo or in a partnership, the look of the dancing body had to be unforced and individual while its shifts of weight maintain a clinically precise concordance with the music in the midst of intricate tapping or linking steps and breathtaking leaps and lifts. In *Saturday Night Fever*'s "Staying Alive," all Tony Manero has to worry about is getting down the street without messing up the pulse or mussing his glossy pompadour. Later, when he and his partner (Karen Lynn Gorney) are in a dance competition, they have more complicated choreographic concerns; but much as their poses and the pompadour excite our admiration, their Mustang is no match for the Astaire-Rogers Duesenberg.

At the Academy Awards on Tuesday, April 7, 1970, Astaire appeared on stage in a tux, with Bob Hope, to announce the prizes for documentaries. He was a mere lad of seventy-one, and obviously spry, but Hope teased him about retiring. Then, suddenly, Hope signaled the conductor to strike up the band, whose rhythms sent Astaire into a lighter version of the crazy-leg solo he performed in the break section of *Follow the Fleet*'s "Let Yourself Go," back in 1936. Go septuagenarians! April 1970 was quite a month for dance. During daytime hours of the eighteenth and nineteenth of that month, choreographer Trisha Brown—a native of the Pacific Northwest who trained with various teachers in various dance genres, among them the Bay Area mother of postmodern dance, Anna Halprin—sent the dancer Joseph Schlichter, then Brown's husband, to step off a roof and, thanks to a harness contraption that kept him from giving in to gravity, proceed to walk down seven stories of the brick-faced SoHo building they lived in, his body at a ninety-degree angle to the wall and parallel to the sidewalk below. As he stepped, he had no options to shift his journey beyond the edges of a narrow path flanked on both sides by metal shutters from apartment windows. No films, but some photos were taken. It is estimated that an audience of some forty persons all together watched.

One of Brown's "equipment pieces" of the period—which included *Walking on the Wall* for seven dancers (1971) and her solo *Woman Walking Down a Ladder* (1973)—this ur-wall-walk from 1970 is known as *Man Walking Down the Side of a Building*. Postings on YouTube show that, in the nearly half century since, it has been frequently revived around the country, but it seems never to be revived intact. For one thing, the walkers are always descending institutional walls that are entirely free of obstructions, so if the walker and attendant harnesses and cable drift a little to the left or right, the walker's ankles won't be assaulted by metal shutters. On the other hand, some of the posted revivals show the walkers having to make their way down many more stories than a mere seven. Footwear also varies. One man wears Birkenstocks; two women each wear what look like combat boots. The unidentified young man at the Walker Art Center of Minneapolis takes the performance in a stately manner, carefully advancing opposite arm to lead leg; a woman at the University of Washington, in Seattle, practically races down her vast wall.

Everyone is tethered to equipment of tremendous bulk and presence; one can practically smell the signatures inked on the contracts for lawyers and insurance companies.

My favorite YouTube revival posting, though, is the brave and imperfect try by the self-described "extreme-action" choreographer and MacArthur "Genius" grant recipient Elizabeth Streb, at the former Whitney Museum, on the Upper East Side of New York. Having seen her and her company at close range in her Brooklyn studio and in the intimate Joyce Theater—where they risk life and limb for their experiments in defying gravity ("A question like: Can you fall up? This is the bedrock of my process," Streb has explained)—I thought that *Man Walking Down the Side of a Building* would be a piece of cake for her. But she visibly had trouble with it, the harnesses and cables notwithstanding. For one thing, she was uncertain at the first step off the roof, bracing her legs too widely and resisting the plunge into the walking rhythm that gave the other solo walkers their crucial momentum, their ignition; and during her walk she veered from side to side, laboring to remain upright in any version of a forward journey. She completed the full walk without needing to be rescued, but she never recovered aplomb.

Afterward, however, she marvelously analyzed the problems in a post that illuminates Brown's work itself. Streb had prepared for her walk by going to the gym and doing sit-ups and back extensions, but that strength training turned out to be irrelevant to this assignment. The key to the walk, she discovered in doing it, was her balance. "I was on the head of a pin," she said. "Every step changed my center." The effect of *Man Walking Down the*

Side of a Building was to deconstruct walking, the everyday movement that most of us take for granted, and, in the deconstruction, to make the walker and the audience recognize how amazing the act of walking is—the same thing Astaire's audiences recognize though through very different means. As Streb spoke, I thought of an observation made about walking in animated films by Marge Champion, a star dancer of Broadway and Hollywood and, as a teenager, the live-action reference for Walt Disney's Snow White. Champion said about the animation of the prince in Disney's masterpiece that it is very hard to "ground" an animated character who is walking, to give the sense of leg and foot first resisting gravity and then giving into it while advancing the entire body. As it turned out, there wasn't quite enough time before the premiere of *Snow White and the Seven Dwarfs* in 1938 to ground the prince as he walked so that the audience could feel him walking; when you study him, he seems to fly off-center a little. If you can walk, you can dance, as long as you understand that the key to both activities is the centering of the body at the core.

Ballet is often spoken of as a kind of dance that defies gravity; "Classic Ballet: Aria of the Aerial," Lincoln Kirstein titled an essay on the subject in 1976. I never quite understood that point of view. One uses gravity to leap; the resistance is crucial to the take-off and the landing. Gravity gives the leap physical meaning. Even dancers with fantastical elevation, such as Natalia Osipova, project their supernatural effects of flying and floating thanks to the way they descend from the air (in ballet, their ballon). Astronauts released from gravity can float, but they can't give the effect of that supernatural, momentary freedom from the laws of physics; the constrictions of time and gravity are what make the theatrical floating an excitement.

The literal defiance of gravity on earth, in the sense of defying the *laws* of gravity—whether the context is to entertain by creating an illusion of ease or to educate with a severely stripped-down, transparent analysis of effort—requires not only a willing defier but also masses of equipment, a team, engineering, patient know-how to experiment, a special location, and on and on. And that is what Fred Astaire and Trisha Brown had in common— the dream of telling Newton to take a hike, a taste for working out the logistics to realize it, and the perseverance to realize it so that it's interesting to observe. Ironically, with the Astaire number, the effects of ease and magic he was aiming for are not what prompted the main questions from fans. They didn't want to learn about why Astaire wanted the effect as much as they wanted to know how the effect was achieved. With Brown, by contrast, as her major photographers demonstrated, many watchers were less interested in the logistics of the harnesses and cables than the magic of the illusions one could enjoy when the equipment pieces were viewed from certain prescribed angles. Peter Moore's photos of Schlichter in *Man Walking Down the Side of a Building* convert the look of the walk from weird experiment to an image of a person walking down a gentle incline; Moore's print also shows a white rope or cable alongside the walker but nothing being attached to Schlicter, who seems to float toward us unaided on a sloping road. And Babette Mangolte's photos of Brown in *Woman Walking Down a Ladder* are even more mysterious, especially the view taken from the side of the ladder (perched just below a water tower on a tenement roof), where the daylight bleaches away any trace of tethering cables, suggesting that the walker is angled ninety degrees to the ladder, descending the steps of it without any human or mechanical assistance, like a medieval saint triumphing over her instrument of torture, thanks to the Divine.

The most spectacular example of walking as a performance in my lifetime occurred early in the morning of August 7, 1974: Philippe Petit—twenty-four-year-old wire walker, juggler, and philosopher—used a crossbow to shoot a one-hundred-ten-foot, one-inch-wide steel cable—or wire—between the rooftops of the Twin Towers (also known as the World Trade Center). He then stepped onto the wire with his wire walking pole for balance and, for fifty minutes, proceeded not only to cross from the north to the south tower roofs but also to cross back, to lie down on the wire, to sit on it so as to gaze down the thirteen hundred feet to the pavement and "take a [mental] photograph" of the crowds looking like ants, to bow to the distant crowds twice, and, essentially, to dance. At last, at the shouted news from his friend on a tower rooftop that the police intended to pick up Petit with a helicopter, Petit decided to obey the shouted threat of a member of the NYPD, also on a tower roof, that if Petit didn't come back in from the wire, the policeman was going to "come out and get him." Petit remarked later that the police insistence on him stopping probably saved his life, as, cavorting on the wire, he had the thought that whatever gods exist may have been growing annoyed and that, as in the myth of Icarus, he wouldn't escape a dark conclusion to his own arrogance. "During the walk I had a sense of dancing on top of the world," Petit remembered in an interview years later, and he recalled that his dance improvisations on high included his lying down full out on the wire and seeing a bird eyeball him as an intruder to the bird's territory. When taken to the police station to be charged with a variety of violations, Petit was asked, "Why did you do it??" He was filmed answering, "I don't know." But decades later, in August 2018, he said on camera for the television show *Inside Edition,* "I was shocked by that [question]! I'm a wire walker!!" He added in explanation, "I see three oranges and I have to juggle them. I see two towers and I have to walk between them." His risk-taking was, for him, an innate response to the world's call to his very identity: the question of "why" was, for him, unanswerable.

But not the question of "how." I don't mean the long-term planning with the crossbow and evading security and so forth; I mean, how did he not get dizzy, scared, and lose his balance? There are individuals who lack the ability to feel fear; they can prove courageous heroes or sociopaths. But Petit does not seem to be one of them. He told one of his interviewers that he was afraid; however, his need to satisfy his impulse for the wire walk exceeded that primal emotion. He spoke of having a mental filter, which permitted him to block out everything about his external and interior environments that might prevent him from focusing on the wire walk at hand. The police were entranced. Instead of hitting him with jail and fines, the authorities asked him to come back and perform for the public in a less dizzying location, such as Central Park. It took him a week to think that over; he came back.

I was not in New York City when Petit took his walk, but it took place so early in the morning (7:00 a.m.) that most of the city learned about it the way I did—through the news at first and later through his meditative interview responses, his book *To Reach the Clouds* (2002), and James Marsh's documentary film *Man on a Wire.* (The title may refer simply to the bird that Petit saw, but it also may be a play on the late 1960s Leonard Cohen song "Bird on the Wire": "Like a bird on the wire / Like a drunk in a midnight choir / I have tried in my way to be free.") Unlike Trisha Brown's *Man Walking Down the Side of a Building,* however, Petit's stunt, or performance, or literalization of a spiritual ascent is a dance in the old-fashioned sense—with changes of position and location and mood—as well as a postmodern experiment in excelsis. As Sergeant Charles Daniels, the policeman interviewed in the documentary, said, it was a once-in-a-lifetime event, and he still seemed stunned by it as he remembered it. "Officer Muñoz and I observed the tightrope dancer," he added, "because you couldn't call him a walker."

In a book on the subject of why dance matters, or can matter, I feel it relevant to mention that Philippe Petit's wire-walking dance not only brought together the Twin Towers in a literal way but also, in the shocking thrill the event continues to inspire in retrospect, it momentarily united in stunned awe an economically distressed and polarized New York City. Subsequent images of those Towers from 9/11 are searing embodiments of what "reality" can mean on a monstrous scale, yet Petit's dance in the clouds, while horror slumbered, was also, for fifty minutes, reality.

5 a florilegium

Senta Driver, a modern dancer, is about to begin a fourteen-minute solo called *Memorandum*. It is 1976, and she no longer dances for Paul Taylor's company (where she performed between 1967 and 1973). Harry, the name of the company she is forming to dance her own choreography, is in the offing. She wears a simple jump-suit and a small veil. Her strong, arched, bare feet take a parallel position—very modern-dance. Unfurling a balletic port de bras upward with both arms, she lifts the veil to show her face. Her hands, now low and pressed together, like a member of the medieval clergy, she takes a step, then another, and another, clock-wise into the circle she will inscribe on the performing space many times, emphasizing her heel-first contact with the floor. Drawing out the vowels, she utters, "Marie Taglioni," the first of many names she will announce—as if at a graduation ceremony—of nineteenth- and twentieth-century ballerinas, mostly European and Russian although with one American (the Philadelphian Augusta Maywood) and one name of a danseur—Vaslav Nijinsky. At "Pierina Legnani" (famous for her bravura fouetté turns), Driver throws her arms heavenward in acclaim. For the three young-teenager "baby ballerinas," whom Balanchine "discovered" in the 1930s, Driver runs their names together as one ("TatianaRiabouchinskaTamaraToumanovaIrinaBaronova"). You hear the names of the Paris Opéra Ballet étoiles from the Serge Lifar years, and a roster of Bolshoi stunners beginning with Galina Ulanova, and a Kirov Alla Sizova here, a La Scala Carla Fracci there. Her pronunciations are studiously correct; and all the while, steadily and surely yet without breaking stride, Driver continues to plow the circle with her footsteps—the circle we can practically feel, the Euclidean geometry that is the basis of classical ballet schooling—here described by a modern dancer. At the last name, "Natalia Makarova," Driver takes a balance on one leg: finis.

Among the countless tributes I know of to ballet of the nineteenth and twentieth centuries, this is not only the simplest but also, by my lights, one of the most thoughtful, synthesizing tradition, memory, variety within repetition, the tension between reliability and surprise that leads one back to a work of art, and—dare I say it?—fun.

I saw Driver live in her *Memorandum* once, in 1976, in a small

New York theater, and it is one of two postmodern solos that have haunted me since I began to write about dance. Both comprised a few, clear elements and both unfolded a simple narrative. My memory is not as good as the above description suggests: there exists an archival film of *Memorandum* at New York's Library for Performing Arts, which enabled me to get the list of names right and to mention the veil, which I'd forgotten.

Of course, you want to know what was in the other solo. There is no film of it that I know of. I do remember that it was made and performed by a performance artist from Myanmar, and I could probably reproduce it with my own body today, although, given my age and with this unconditioned body—the young man who performed it looked to be in his twenties and as thin as a kris—I wouldn't sell any tickets. There is no sound score other than the ambient sounds in the room where you are. A vision in black from hair to shoe soles, you walk purposefully onto your stage with, in one hand, a folding chair, which you open and then sit down on. In your other hand, you hold a roll of duct tape and a pair of scissors. From somewhere on your person, you take out a hood of black fabric and put it over your head. By feel, you attach the accessible end of the tape to the lower third of the hood and start to encircle your hooded head with it, making sure that with each revolution the tape is positioned over your mouth, which is open. You encircle your head many times. Finally, also by feel, you take the scissors and cut the tape, being sure that the cut edge is pasted flat. You pause for a moment so the audience can take in the image. Then, from either a pants pocket or waistband, you produce a small revolver. With deliberation, you bring the barrel to point directly into the center of the indentation where your taped-over open mouth is. You pull the trigger. There is a sound of a shot. Blackout. A study in minimalism, its movement deliberately untheatrical, the piece was so understated as to be banal—except that it was a bucket of ice water to witness and remains memorable twenty years later.

When I decided to bring that performance into this book I dug around on Google and found some information about it. The evening was part of an Asian Performance Art Festival at the Japan Society, given the eighteenth and nineteenth of October 2001, that is, a little over one month after 9/11. Performers from Japan, Indonesia, Korea, Thailand, and Vietnam made their U.S. debuts on the program. The man with the chair and prop gun was Aye Ko, a visual artist from Myanmar, an art critic and writer, and the then-director of Yangon's New Zero Art Space. Born in 1963, he had been a painter until 1996, when he converted his energies to performance art. His appearance in New York seems to have been part of a world tour he was making in the United States, Indonesia, and China, with an estimated return to Myanmar in 2007. I wonder if he completed it. In the event, his piece remains for me one frontier to explain what dance is decidedly not.

Memorandum could also be debated as an example of minimalism in performance, although, in view of the competition for lean-and-mean minimalism posed by the Burmese artist, perhaps Driver's work could be said to be maximalist minimalism. In the event, it is also the first dance I remember seeing of which I was strongly aware that it was built on walking and that the walking, in tandem with the dancer's gestures and songlike articulation of the names of ballerinas, verged on transforming itself from transportation into dancing while keeping its street cred as performance art. During the pandemic year, I finally reached out to Senta Driver to ask about how *Memorandum* was made, and why. The depth of thought and craft that I'd felt was present in this Judson-era choreography turned out to run deeper than I could have imagined. "Walking!" she said right away. "It's the first thing you do." She went on:

When I came into the field, it was people making wonderful new proposals, and they all clashed. I thought that's what you were supposed to do, new ideas, new aesthetics. I went into a studio and, walking, put my foot on every inch of the floor for three hours a day. I was *finding* things, like in a lab. I also thought I was finding a new movement vocabulary. I'd had no ballet at all. I started studying dance at Bryn Mawr, where I majored in Latin and Medieval Studies. [She also studied modern dance at Connecticut College, Ohio State University, and, for a summer, Jacob's Pillow, where she did encounter "some Margaret Craske Ballet."] [But] I was too old for ballet, and my physique was not suitable.

The walk is a stride on the heels. I was making a sound with my feet. I felt I was making a piece you could *hear*. I became attached to the sound on my heels. It was like composing, not structures but sequences according to vocal music. I was very inspired by people who did a cappella madrigals and singing. I chose the names because of the pronunciation. I had myself schooled to the accurate pronunciation. I brought in an actress to give me notes. For example, the name "Price" [the Royal Danish Ballet Bournonville ballerina Ellen Price, 1878–1968], in Danish, is pronounced "PREE-sah."

Driver also noted something I was unlikely to have guessed from watching alone: her development of the walk emphasizing her heels was not an intentional cue that she was a modern dancer in this world of ballet references. It was, rather, an opposition to another modern dancer—to Martha Graham, whose choreographed walks emphasized the pointed foot. With this, Driver reminded me that there are always more things in heaven and earth than are dreamed of in my (or any dance critic's) philosophy. One can think of Hamlet's caveat to Horatio in a couple of ways. If one is dispirited, then it means one will never entirely solve the puzzle, account for everything in one's interpretation, or even perceive everything there might be to perceive—that the dance will never be truly knowable, one's devoted efforts notwithstanding, and that one will always be Horatio, never Hamlet, even in one's own story of one's life. On the other hand, it could also mean that there is always room in a study of dance for one's individual intuition or imagination. (This entire book is built on the strength of that second hand.)

What follows is my subjective gathering of some of the most beautiful examples I know, and have not yet discussed, of works where choreographers have used walking to illuminate dancing, in ways that are deeply meaningful and affecting, works I return to again and again, always finding something fresh to ponder. For the most part, walking is something quite special in them—an element of seriousness, of meditation, of the sacred, of deep reflection, of memory. Sometimes, the dancing figures are characters who are conscious of the distinction between walking and dancing. It is a small and quite incomplete niche list of works I love.

The Walking Chorus from *L'Allegro, il Penseroso, ed il Moderato*

L'Allegro, Mark Morris's full-evening, two-act suite of dances to a vocal score by G. F. Handel using versions of poems by John Milton, is more or less universally considered to be one of the masterpieces of twentieth-century theatrical dance. On a *Great Performances* program for PBS, Morris spoke about the great ensemble section he calls the Walking Chorus because much of it is given over to its lines of twenty-four dancers walking in geometric formations, not unlike those for the horse ballets of the Renaissance. In fact, Morris describes their tread as a "limping step, up-down up-down, like posting on a horse." He adds, "It looks great from anywhere. It's meant to make people want to participate."

Morris, who considers himself a musician who makes dances, studied ballet, flamenco, and other dance traditions when he was growing up, but the dance experience that seems to have most impressed him in youth was his participation in Koleda Balkan Dance Ensemble, a folk dance group in his native Seattle that flourished from 1967 to 1974. The Walking Chorus rings continually surprising changes on the line dances and intricate geometric figures of folk dances from Greece and eastern Europe. Other dance or dancelike references may spring to mind: some dancegoers might be led to remember the harvesters' crossing-line dances in *Giselle,* and some gamers might be prompted to think of Pac-Man, and some academics might suggest an analogy from political philosophy—a united social contract in a true democracy at peace with itself because its participants, who often can't agree on the time of day, are at one with their core purpose, that is, the honoring of their common music. The irony, of course, is that to achieve the theatrical effects that prompt these musings requires a choreographer who is an absolute monarch.

Walkings on Pointe

Bournonville's version of this ballet is the second; the original was *La Sylphide* choreographed by Filippo Taglioni, to different music, in 1832 for his daughter, Marie, then a sensation at the Paris Opéra Ballet owing to her airy grace and her dancing on pointe, in shoes that were stiffened by no more than a few embroidery threads on the outside of the toes and a bit of cardboard on the inside. The strength of her feet and the placement of her spine, resulting from the dancer's iron discipline over countless hours, were the tough, boring secrets of her incandescent effects. It could even be said that she had the wrong body for her profession, with ill-proportioned arms and a face that wasn't especially pretty. (Inherent physical attractiveness, so important to a career in the dance theater for the past century, where film set the standard, was not a requirement for stardom in nineteenth-century ballet.) Taglioni's James was Joseph Mazilier, not only a dancer with the Opéra but also the choreographer of the popular original productions of *Paquita* (1844) and *Le Corsaire* (1856). Their choreography has mostly been lost—indeed, none of Mazilier's ballets survived as more than fragments. The loss of Taglioni's version of *La Sylphide* was business as usual (though, in the 1970s,

Pierre Lacotte did attempt to reconstruct it from documents and, surely, retrospective guessing via the Danish version). The *Sylphide* of Bournonville, however, has been essentially preserved from its beginning.

(An aside: Dance works are preserved because dancers enjoy dancing them, not because they create a sensation in their time or because critics do or do not like them. It is one of the open secrets of dance history that, after the tempest over Nijinsky's *Rite of Spring* at its first preview performance, audiences actually quieted down and paid attention. "At first acquaintance, this ballet was so completely novel in its outlook, so starkly primitive in its conception, so brutal in its movements, that many found it utterly repellent," wrote the historian Cyril Beaumont, who attended, it appears, at least three of the six performances that constituted the *Rite*'s entire life cycle. "But after the first shock had passed, and the ballet had been witnessed a second and a third time, it was seen to possess much primitive beauty and to evoke a deep inner emotion." Dance historians—and the team of *Rite* reconstructors, Millicent Hodson and Kenneth Archer—have tried to remind popular writers of Beaumont's point, but the excitement of the original ruckus and scandal has overpowered Beaumont's sensitive and informed reporting in popular retellings. There were surely practical reasons why Diaghilev didn't keep Nijinsky's *Rite* in repertory. But the likeliest reason that Nijinsky's choreography was scrapped is that the dancers disliked performing it.)

It may be that the moment I'm isolating was one that Bournonville remembered rather than created—that it had been in Taglioni's *Sylphide* first. Whichever was the case, in my words here it is:

It's James Ruben's wedding day with Effie, but a Sylph has flown into the farmhouse from the forest and fallen in love with James, mischievously luring him away from his fiancée. At one point, early on, everyone but James has gone to prepare for the wedding. He is daydreaming of the Sylph. Suddenly, the casement window opens and there she is, just outside the hall. She steps over the sill and down a step or two into the room. She and James are falling in love; as this happens, they walk forward in tandem towards the audience—he on the soles of his feet and she on the tips of her toes. This walk only lasts for a few seconds, but it is taken with high solemnity, and, at a flash, as they perform what seem like identical actions, their walking foreshadows their differences, which will destroy them individually.

The passage is an image of distinction within similarity that, so to speak, has legs. You can find a version of it in a Marius Petipa ballet, performed by a ballerina stepping on pointe while holding the hand of her best-friend ballerina who is walking on flat, each of their footfalls tracing one of the opposing edges of a long ribbon of flowers. This takes place in the sumptuous vision scene, known as "Le Jardin Animé," which beautifies Petipa's version from 1899 (his last of four) of his four-act spectacle *Le Corsaire,* which Alexei Ratmansky and Yuri Burlaka revived, using archival sources, for the Bolshoi Ballet in 2007. The two ballerinas are the work's principal female characters, Medora and Gulnare; Medora is more central to the story, and so she is the member of the sisterly pair who walks on pointe. The prestige of the shoe translates to a hierarchy of class. In this context, though, as figures in someone else's dream, the walking pair have no control over their destinies. There is no tragic distinction between them as they are, together, enslaved in a harem. The potential for tragedy lies elsewhere in this comic ballet.

By the time of Balanchine's surrealist Sleepwalker, a half century later, the theatrical idea of two different kinds of shoes to represent not only sexual but also moral difference has become rather complex. Balanchine maintains the emotional hierarchy of the pointe shoe for the central Sleepwalker ballerina. (There is a second ballerina—the Coquette—also in pointe shoes; she is the Sleepwalker's nemesis and, ultimately, the agent of the Poet's death. To my knowledge, Balanchine never paired ballerinas unless both were on pointe.) However, when the Poet partners the ballerina-Sleepwalker, she walks at different rates, as if to gauge internal excitement, while he walks, runs, and practically turns himself inside-out to get her to acknowledge him, going so far as to roll on the ground and then bend himself backward in two; still, nothing he does can prevent her from, inexorably, walking over his outstretched arms. In the case of this world of the *Night Shadow* (from 1946, revived in 1960 as *La Sonnambula*), the beauty and prestige of walking on pointe have become estranged from everyday life, rendering the Sleepwalker numinous in the context of the cruel reality in which she is immured. Even so, her skimming pointes also retain something of the Sylph's quality as an untouchable ideal in the world of imagination, where Sleepwalker and Poet cannot connect physically yet meet intuitively.

Le défilé at Paris

The year is 1926. Léo Staats, the artistic director of the Paris Opéra Ballet—and a neoclassical choreographer whose purity of taste during the 1920s anticipated works by Ashton and Balanchine in the 1930s and 1940s—creates a gala formal presentation of the hundreds of dancers in the Opéra's ballet company and school. From start to finish, it takes a quarter of an hour to complete. Called simply *Le défilé,* it was performed only twice before World War II, and the accompaniment was Richard Wagner's march from *Tannhäuser.* In 1945—the war having ended and the Paris Opéra Ballet in disorder with the removal of its ballet master Serge Lifar, charged with being a Nazi collaborator during the Occupation of Paris—the dancer, choreographer, and ballet master Albert Aveline, whose career at the ballet began in 1894, when he entered the school, was brought back for a time to head the company. During this brief period, he reinstated what had been *Le défilé,* naming it *Le grand défilé* and staging it, in its third performance ever, to the more palatable March of the Trojans from Hector Berlioz's opera *Les Troyens.* (Aveline also introduced the Romantic-style costumes for the male dancers, which are still in use.)

Mixing military precision of execution with an imperial presentation, the procession today is a dazzling display of the theater's (and, by extension, the state's) human treasure. It opens with one little girl from the school, rising like a naiad from a reclining position on the floor, to become a cadet of art before our eyes. Her step—an arrowing dégagé, which transforms her leg into a tiny instrument of war against indiscipline, ending in a fierce point—is repeated by all the dancers who follow her, each fastidiously placing every footfall on an invisible line in front of the center of the body. They advance in waves: the other female students arranged according to age, the female corps de ballet and various soloists of the company, the ballerina étoiles, presented individually, who are allowed to break from the formal walk into a run to meet their applauding audience and bow deeply, and then all the boys and men and male étoiles. With the run, they become "real." At the end, all the dancers assemble themselves to form a living sculpture of a life-sized baroque horseshoe, mirroring the architecture of the theater.

The Australian dance writer Michelle Potter (a past curator of the Jerome Robbins Dance Division at the New York Public Library for the Performing Arts at Lincoln Center) described the event this way on April 19, 2015, on her blog, . . . *on dancing:*

> Opening the program was the Paris Opera Ballet's traditional parade of dancers from the company and its school—the *défilé*— seen for the first time on film. This spectacular presentation begins in a chandeliered ante-room, the *foyer de la danse* of Degas fame. Some 350 artists and artists-to-be, beginning with the youngest children from the ballet school and ending with the *étoiles* of the company, make their way from the ante-room down the stage of the Palais Garnier, giving a bow as they reach the front of the stage before moving into assigned places. There is no formal dancing as such but it generates goose-bumps to see these dancers on parade, and to hear the audience honour them with, as might be expected, the greatest applause given to the *étoiles,* who enter singly rather than in a group as happens with the rest of the artists. Finally they form a tableau which Robert Greskovic has described in his book

Ballet 101: a complete guide to learning and loving the ballet: "In its final tableau the *défilé* amasses a garden of ballet beauty, paying homage to the art form's continuity and freshness."

Rhythm Tap

Practically the entire art form is based on the exchange of weight in an upright body that begins with, and rings (often elaborate) changes on, walking. The pride of being able to generate sound so evenly with each foot that someone listening wouldn't be able to discern if the dancer was on the left foot or the right—as in the stair dances of Bill Robinson (1878–1949)—is a standard of execution derived from walking as an action. From that bipedalism, the art of tap dancing goes all over the map: into heel-dropping (John Bubbles), off to asymmetry (Baby Laurence [Laurence Donald Jackson]), to asymmetry onto the toes (the Nicholas Brothers), sliding across the floor (Jimmy Slyde), to a bel canto clarity of sound (Dianne "Lady Di" Walker), to delicate rhythmic complications (Dormeshia). When the hulking figure of the great dancer Chuck Green (1919–1997) performed his signature "A Train" dance to the Duke Ellington–Billy Strayhorn tune, he included a feathery jump directly upward whose energy lifted his body like helium, including his gaze: one saw the whites of his eyes. (The first time I saw him do this, I thought it was improvised, but he danced the same at every performance of the number.) The paddle-and-roll steps of Bunny Briggs (1922–2014) carry the ambulation one stage further, so that the dancer seemed to be walking on water, as if each foot were shod in a little jet ski.

The greased moonwalking of Michael Jackson isn't tap, but its effect as a vernacular dance move links it to some of tap's effects. It has a strange, almost melancholic quality: the dancer looks forward but the walking body, automatonically, insists on taking him backward, and he appears to lack any way to reverse that insistence. At the other end of dance consciousness is Savion Glover (b. 1973), whose command of his body's ability to make the most complex sounds in the business is such that he can stand in place, seemingly still, seemingly with both feet placed on the floor, and his feet will be declaiming monologues, using every part of his shoes, including the outer rims, to produce—without any part of him visibly moving—a universe of sound.

Frederick Ashton's Elgar and Turgenev

Ashton's period ballet *Enigma Variations (My Friends Pictured Within)*, from 1968, and his *A Month in the Country*, of 1976, are masterpieces of continuous transformation between drama and dance, and the deepest emotions are in the passages where the characters unemphatically weave walking into dancing and back. Walking characters begin and conclude *A Month in the Country*, based on Ivan Turgenev's play and set to John Lanchbery's arrangements of Chopin; and the gestures that Ashton devised are so apt for the situation that "dancing" and "real life" lose their borders. When, as the curtain falls on *Month*, Natalia paces directly forward toward us, as if she's going to pass across the lip of the stage over the orchestra pit and into the house, she embodies Ashton's memory of Isadora Duncan, whom he saw when he was at the sunrise of his career and she was edging toward the sunset of hers. He loved her directness, the honesty of her movement. His broken-hearted Natalia, a part built for the great dancer-actress Lynn Seymour, holds the opera house by herself, Isadora-fashion, as, the curtain falling, she advances into the end of her youth as if to a scaffold.

The most persuasive writing I know of about the Nimrod Variation of Ashton's *Elgar* is a paragraph by Joan Acocella, published on August 2, 2004, within a comment titled "Life Steps," in the *New Yorker*. It accounts for both the dance action and the poetic implications of that action—that is, for what physical facts can be perceived and what associations they might suggest.

> The composer is seen in a dark time. He feels ignored by the public. He doubts his gifts, and amid the bustle in his household he stands alone, pensive. Near the middle of the ballet his solitude is spotlighted in an unforgettable dance called the "Nimrod Variation," where he takes a walk with his friend and publisher, A. J. Jaeger. Elgar said that the music for this variation was a memory of a "summer evening's talk about Beethoven" between the two men. In a ballet you can't talk, so what Ashton's two dancers do is mostly walk, interspersing their paces with slow, plangent gestures. They turn outward from each other, then back inward. They do ronds de jambe par terre, in which the foot traces a circle on the floor. This, I suppose, is their ratiocination, the discussion of Beethoven that—these being men, and Victorian men—both disguises and contains their feelings for each other. Soon they are joined by Elgar's wife, and the men pass her back and forth between them, in low lifts. She becomes the stand-in for Beethoven, the medium through which the two friends speak to each other. The dance is very austere, particularly compared with the welling music that accompanies it, and it ends as modestly as it

began, with the three dancers simply lifting their arms to Heaven, as if asking a question. The subject is sympathy, meaning not just fellow feeling but the separateness we have to bridge—and that we never bridge except partially—to get into the mind of another person, however loved. No other ballet choreographer has examined normal emotions with such sophistication.

Dances to Music by J. S. Bach

Is it the walking-bass line of baroque music that inspires choreographers to employ the act of walking so often in the presence of music by J. S. Bach? Balanchine's *Concerto Barocco* of 1941—set to the Double Violin Concerto in D Minor and considered an example of ballet architecture to be classified among the greatest works of Western art in any medium—features walking throughout its second movement ("Largo ma non tanto" is the musical direction), for both its corps de ballet of eight women and its principal male dancer, who partners one of the work's two ballerinas by assisting her in several unexpected drops and recoveries and in a series of sailing lifts from side to side until she comes to rest on the pointe of one foot in arabesque. Holding her hand, he accompanies her in fast runs and complex sculptural interactions with the dancers around her, who seem both spirits who serve her and whom she blesses by her presence. Some very interesting dance writing and scholarship has addressed this ballet. Much of it is concerned with the two outer movements (marked "Vivace" and "Allegro"), the last movement especially, where Balanchine divides the corps in half and sets them to perform a kind of classical tap in counterpoint. (During the 1930s, Balanchine did choreograph jazz dancing for Josephine Baker and the Nicholas Brothers and he worked on Broadway shows and Hollywood movies with various tap consultants.) Kara Yoo Leaman, a professor of music at Oberlin College and Conservatory, has published an extensive (and much discussed) analysis of the way the third-movement choreography relates to the music.

But the second movement does not seem to capture these writers' imaginations as it did Edwin Denby's, who reviewed the ballet's first two New York performances for the *Herald Tribune*. It was in the second review that we find the much-quoted metaphorical passage that Denby—an influential poet as well as a dancer, choreographer, and critic—developed about trees in the wind (perhaps an image evoked by the dancers running?), with the image of the lone danseur, after lifting and lowering the ballerina to this side then that side then this side, suspensefully bringing her stiffened leg and pointed toe to a pose in arabesque, placing her supporting pointe on the stage in such a deliberate conclusion to an impassioned sequence that it left the impression, to Denby, of a blade plunging into a wound. Even if Denby's vision no longer haunts the performance practice of current productions, no longer tightens the arcs of the lifts and the timing of the lowering, to me it is still as intrinsic to that second movement as the shadow sought by Peter Pan. Marie-Jeanne, the original ballerina who was lifted, noted that Balanchine slowed the tempo of the Largo section in 1948, when NYCB was established, and so the imagery that Denby saw and felt originally at a cutting speed was dissipated. Such technical changes, such details of logistics, can make the most dramatic of differences in dance, especially for someone whose idea of any given ballet contains levels and layers of its composition and performance history.

Happily, Balanchine attracts many devoted and imaginative knights. Nancy Reynolds, the research director of the George Balanchine Foundation, has given the world some of the most valuable books, interviews, and video programs concerning the work of this choreographer over time. The searing practical criticism of Arlene Croce (couched in matchlessly crafted declarative sentences), the heart-catching analyses of individual ballets by Nancy Goldner, the generous and impeccable chronicle of Balanchine's teaching by Suki Schorer, much of the massive and ranging oeuvre of Lincoln Kirstein, and the many loving, keenly observant memoirs by Balanchine's dancers and admirers provide a comprehensive portrait of a ballet master enjoyed, at least in English, by no other figure in theatrical dance. Still, there seems to be no end to discoveries. The musicologist James Steichen, for instance, has performed diligent research in the Performing Arts Library that has yielded, among other surprises, an explanation of why, in his will, Balanchine gave the rights for his Bach ballet *Concerto Barocco* to Kirstein, whose idea it may have been, and an unexpected skein of connections among that work, the classical tap dancing of Paul Draper, and Balanchine's dances for the Rodgers and Hart show *On Your Toes*. At first, I resisted Steichen's conclusions; however, I returned to the library and put myself through his research process. To my astonishment, he convinced me.

A book that offers yet more revelations concerning the art of Balanchine and his dancers is Martha Ullman West's meticulous *Todd Bolender, Janet Reed, and the Making of American Ballet*

(2021). West, who interviewed extensively the dancer and choreographer Todd Bolender—a member of Balanchine's performing companies during the 1940s and 1950s—lets us look through the window of Bolender's hitherto-unpublished recollections, for instance, that Balanchine made *Concerto Barocco* in part to showcase the empyrean, quicksilver technique of Marie-Jeanne, who, at the age of fifteen, "could perform *entrechat huit* too fast to count them." Yet West also tracks Bolender's perspective as a choreographer on Balanchine's work. Of *Concerto Barocco* and another masterpiece from 1941, *Ballet Imperial,* he says that they marked a new stage for Balanchine, one he had been working toward for some time. For Bolender, *Barocco* "has an importance that puts it into a class completely removed from any other Balanchine ballet with the possible exception of *Four Temperaments.* [I]t obviously was composed by one as deeply in love with music as with movement." West suggests that *Barocco* may have been unlike any other Balanchine work in a different way, too. Her demonic research rediscovered an interview given to Nancy Reynolds, in 1976, by the composer and peerless musical arranger for dance Trude Rittmann, an émigré from Nazi Germany who worked with Virgil Thomson, Leonard Bernstein, Aaron Copland, Agnes de Mille, and many others. In the interview, Rittmann told Reynolds that she worked with Balanchine on all the counts for the third movement of *Concerto Barocco*—"note by note," "phrase by phrase." An esteemed figure to those in the know in the world of music, Rittmann seems to have comported herself with the same humility that Balanchine expected of his dancers, and so it is quite possible that she was telling the truth about her involvement in the making of *Concerto Barocco.* If she was, her participation does not diminish Balanchine's amazing achievement in that work; to the contrary, it expands one's appreciation for the capaciousness of his intellect—which seems to have had few walls.

Does the walking-bass line of Bach's music evoke choreographers' ongoing concerns with the human act of walking? This was the case for Paul Taylor, who was known among his dancers for his belief in the revelatory powers of a person's gait and for asking applicants in auditions to walk so that he could see their interior selves displayed (Balzac's "physiognomy of walking" put into practice!). Each of his six Bach dances has moments of walking that tell his audience, Pay attention here! The first section of *Esplanade* embodies this interest when it shifts into the dark second movement. Contrast and change rule this world: walking can be converted to running at the drop of an eyelash, just as unforeseen circumstances can bring forward the bestial origins of humanity. Taylor, in *Esplanade,* is working with portions of the very same Bach Double Violin Concerto in D Minor that Balanchine chose to stage completely in *Concerto Barocco,* yet the modern dancer's reading is so strong that in performance it sends the ballet masterpiece on vacation.

Taylor's evolution as an artist can be mapped in his Bach dances. He made his first, *Junction,* to excerpts from the cello suites, in the early 1960s, when he was still performing with Martha Graham. In a review on April 12, 1986, in the *New York Times,* Jennifer Dunning writes of the dance that it is "pretty, mostly lighthearted . . . an uncompromisingly plotless work, filled with quirks and squiggles, apparent non sequiturs whose unmotivated look is heightened by the stately, pensive walks with which the dance is also filled." (She suggests that its tone may be a kind of resistance to the solemnity of Graham's theater.) Taylor's use of walking in his *Brandenburgs* (1988) as a procession for the lead man and his three attendant muses is meditative, serious, with references (intended or not) to the ending of Balanchine's *Apollo*. It also invokes elegiac offstage ceremonies in memoriam. By *Brandenburgs*, Taylor had learned to fold in the lightness and darkness together to coexist. The walking is stately. In Taylor's last Bach work, *Promethean Fire* (2003), the elements of light and dark have been entirely mixed. *Promethean* is monstrously dark in its look yet soaringly alive in feeling. There is no need in it for revelatory walking, as all has been revealed.

For me, though, the great example of how Taylor used walking as a meditative—even metaphysical—way of thinking through dancing was at the end of a work called *Eventide* (1997). In this dance, set to the suite of the same name by Ralph Vaughan Williams, he created characters, all male-female couples, each highlighted in a duet, inscribing their personality as a dyad through their use of posture and gesture. Through the tempi of their dances as well as their fluent relationships to one another in space, they also give the barest of suggestions as to their stories—not only what the outline of each story is but also where we're seeing the couple in that particular narrative arc, most of which the audience fills in from the constellated hints. One couple, the anchoring pair, have two duets, the first with the man ascendent, the second with the woman in the power position. (Taylor used to tell people that those duets were influenced by the work of Antony Tudor, with whom Taylor had studied at the Juilliard School.) At the end of the dance, all the men line up on a diagonal to face a continuation of the line by all of the women lined up, the difference being that the women are facing the men. And then, in a rocking rhythm, the two lines ebb and flow toward and away from one another, finally to split apart with finality and exit in opposite directions. I happened to see this dance being rehearsed several times, and in the uniform of leotards and tights, it had an abstract gravitas that made me think of the double helix of our DNA. But because the two strands were no longer spiraled around one another—because they were pulling and pulling and then pulled apart—in the company of Vaughan Williams's stately musical conclusion, the effect on me was of the end of life as we know it: I find it the most tragic episode in all the dances by Taylor I have met. Most readers may not be able to find that level of it, though: for, in theatrical performance, you will see the couples costumed, by Santo Loquasto, in period clothing suggestive of springtime in a southern climate and lit, by Jennifer Tipton, in tones suggestive of available light. Still, even in this attractive presentation, underneath is a level of a tragic, implacable end. For me, it is Taylor at his greatest.

The Belgian choreographer Anne Teresa, Baroness De Keersmaeker—trained partially in New York at NYU Tisch, in 1981—may or may not have seen that Bach work of Taylor's. She, like

Taylor, has choreographed for years to J. S. Bach, but her way of responding to the music is very much her own. Her two-hour work *The Six Brandenburg Concertos* (2018), for some sixteen dancers of her company, Rosas, was performed in New York in the vast drill hall of the Park Avenue Armory, and it proved both more like streaming cinema than stage dancing and more abstract than Taylor's choreography; furthermore, no dancers from its ensemble were sequestered or individuated—the way Taylor's *Brandenburgs* quartet is plucked from the whole and given a section of intimacy with the audience. Set in a huge platter, brilliantly lit, the dancers, clad in black, are highly energized, and their balletic modern dance is precise and clear yet also remote; to me, at times, they looked like letters leaping over vellum. In remarks of July 26, 2018, published on the *Rosas* website, De Keersmaeker also, unlike Taylor, pays homage to the composer's religious devotion, noting that Bach "always added the small subscript '*soli deo gloria*' [Glory to God alone] to his scores," but then she speaks of the concertos in musicological rather than reverential terms. And unlike Taylor, who made dances according to counts he devised from the way he himself heard the music—emotionally and imaginatively he related quite personally to Bach—she explains in a cool, impersonal, postmodern way of how she has used the music to make a case for her architectural and structural interests.

> In my own choreographic design, I wanted to pay close attention to the overarching form of Bach's cycle. In the first part of the first concerto, I let the entire group of dancers walk the bassline in *unisono,* following the principle of "My walking is my dancing"—a

theme which I'd already explored in previous performances. Also in *Mitten wir im Leben sind,* I let the dancers literally walk some parts of the bassline that carries the course of the music, making it visible: one note, one step. In the first part of the first Brandenburg Concerto, all dancers walk in a straight line, backwards or forwards, from a frontal perspective. And by using a very simple set of musical canons, I then introduce the first visual counterpoint a while later. . . .

Spurred on by the famous anapest rhythm (short-short-long), which dominates the entire first section, the principle of "my walking is my dancing" then changes into the more audacious principle of "my running is my dancing."

Listening to all six concertos in order can challenge one's concentration, but in the company of De Keersmaeker's limber, kaleidoscopic, and spectacularly lit choreographic figures, not to speak of the passionate account of the music by the B'Rock Orchestra under the baton of violinist Amandine Beyer, whose ideas about the music clearly contributed to this production, the result made this audience member think of watching a loved one undergo brain surgery on a screen one studies from a seat on a working rollercoaster.

Balanchine rarely used J. S. Bach's music over his career. And the one time he set Bach's sacred music, in 1943, he did not make dance. That was "The Crucifixion of Christ" from *The Saint Matthew Passion,* a performance benefitting the American Friends Service Committee, conceived by Leopold Stokowski, Robert Edmond Jones, and Balanchine, who staged the groupings of children from the School of American Ballet as they enacted "a modern form of miracle play" on the stage of the Metropolitan Opera House, with the singers in the pit and Lillian Gish playing Maria Magdalena. For Balanchine, the sacred was the sacred, and ballet was ballet. But our idea of *Concerto Barocco* today, nearly a century after this work first saw the light of a stage, is much smaller, I believe, than Balanchine's idea was when he put the work together. Suki Schorer, from the late 1950s through the early 1970s generation of NYCB dancers, reported that, during a rehearsal, Balanchine asked the cast to make *Concerto Barocco* jazzier, "to use the hip," which bespeaks the choreographer's point of view concerning the Double Violin Concerto in D Minor, to which the ballet is set. The second movement of the ballet—in which the first of two starring ballerinas is partnered in cruising lifts and earthly arabesques as the small female corps walks through a cat's cradle of architectural formations—may look like a small cathedral, and is certainly dignified, but the context is secular: it is dancing in this life—perhaps reminiscent now of the Russian women's folk dance called the *khorovod,* "performed at a walking pace," according to the authoritative *JVC Video Anthology of World Music and Dance* (1990).

In 1941, though, the frames of reference for ballerina Marie-Jeanne, who performed the second movement with William Dollar, and for John Taras, who saw the ballet in the 1940s, were larger than classical ballet alone: they included jazz. When Marie-Jeanne was brought by the George Balanchine Foundation, in 1996, to coach *Concerto Barocco,* she and Taras were interviewed on camera by foundation research director Nancy Reynolds and musicologist Stephanie Jordan, whose outstanding musicological writings and video projects on music and dance have addressed Balanchine ballets. Taras pointed out that a very popular classical and jazz pianist of the early 1940s was the Trinidad-born virtuoso Hazel Scott, who was known for "swinging the classics." Indeed, Scott's Decca recording of that title can be listened to online, and its J. S. Bach selection—Two-Part Invention in A Minor—hurtles through time faster than a speeding locomotive. Furthermore, as Taras emphasized and Marie-Jeanne assented to, the look of the original cast was not the pulled-up, formal, straightened-knee presentation of dancers in recent decades. In the 1940s, Taras said, there were lots of "loose knees." That is, the cast incorporated vernacular dance into their pointe work.

Did the tone of their dancing in *Concerto Barocco* resemble at all that of Katherine Dunham's own dance technique, an amalgam of ballet, modern dance, social dance, and dancing from the Caribbean? Less than a decade later, the technique of Balanchine's New York City Ballet produced dancers who, perhaps thanks to Balanchine's now-regular teaching of company class, made an effort to straighten their knees, which—as Taras and Marie-Jeanne explained—would change a loose rond de jambe à terre (where the leg circles around from front to back) into tendu (the arrowing extension on the floor that returns into one of the academic positions). And both Taras and Marie-Jeanne agreed that how the dancing body was presented in 1941 changed the effect of how the Bach was heard, from music that excites a body already relaxed to respond (the jazz quality) to music that commands dancerly reverence and a formal presentation (the danse d'école). Dance historians Brenda Dixon Gottschild and the late Sally Banes have analyzed the general influence of Black dance on some of Balanchine's mid-career ballets. Was the original look of the slow movement of the *Concerto Barocco* of 1941 evocative in particular of Balanchine's collaboration with Dunham on the Broadway production of *Cabin in the Sky* of 1940? Written accounts by Dunham of the making of the Broadway musical, collected in the Balanchine Foundation's "Popular Balanchine" archive (compiled by the scholar Constance Valis Hill) at the Jerome Robbins Dance Division, speak to the ease and mutual sympathy that Dunham and Balanchine seem to have enjoyed in rehearsal. Balanchine also admired the sophisticated theatricality of the costume and scenic designs of Dunham's husband, John Pratt. The critic Nancy Goldner has observed that the partnering in the second movement of *Barocco* is not romantic, which sets it apart from just about every other known partnered adagio in the Balanchine repertory. The focus is on the ballerina, who seems to drive the action. Was that the nature of Balanchine and Dunham's collaboration on the show, where Balanchine saw his function as both director and choreographer to be, in this rare instance, the protection of Dunham's freedom as a creative artist?

How tempting it is in the arts to constellate associations on the basis of less evidence than a wing and a prayer! The association of Dunham with the principal ballerina figure in the choreographer's creative impulses during the construction of *Concerto Barocco* sounds quite unlikely, yet it's not impossible. Balanchine and Dunham not only collaborated with frictionless ease, according to Dunham, but Balanchine also went to bat for her with a producer: he, so to speak, had her back, just as the male partner in *Barocco*'s Largo ma non troppo section literally has the back of the ballerina in those airborne flights and also in his three restorations of her from deep descents. Balanchine's protectiveness went beyond stage imagery. In one offstage incident on Dunham's behalf, Balanchine even dropped his fabled reserve and, tempting the ultimate devil of vulgarity, declared loudly to a big-wheel meddler where to go. The story is that Balanchine and his friend the Russian expatriate composer Vernon Duke, who wrote the *Cabin* score (and recounted the incident in his memoir), along with the show's designer Boris Aronson, engaged in a mutual explosion against the producer Martin Beck, who wanted Dunham's emotionally expressive dances that were specific to each scene to be removed and replaced by generic yet commercially reliable rhythm tapping. Beck's demands were a final straw, up with which Balanchine—bellowing, as Duke remembered, "This is MY theater! I am the director! YOU get out!"—would not put. The three revolutionaries stomped from the astonished producer's office in a my-way-or-the-highway move—and they won: Dunham and her troupe stayed in the stage picture.

Years later, Dunham still carried a torch for Balanchine's dance making, writing that she wished she, and not Vera Zorina, had performed Balanchine's "That Old Black Magic" dance, to Harold Arlen's song, in the film *Star Spangled Rhythm* (1943), where the dancer, barefoot, steps out of a GI's photograph and streaks, nearly sails, through Hollywood snow. I do not in any way intend to suggest that Dunham had ever replaced Zorina in Balanchine's primary affections or that the star of the *Concerto Ba-*

rocco in 1941 was anyone but Marie-Jeanne. Indeed, who knows who ever is the focus at any given time of anyone's unstated or unrealized affections in the performing arts? What I do intend, though, is to offer the point that when a choreographer concentrates as intently on musical elements as Balanchine did in making *Concerto Barocco* it can temporarily free the part of the creative semiconsciousness where wishes, lies, and dreams are harbored and guarded. When, about two-thirds of the way through the Largo, the second ballerina makes a surprising entrance from a wing, as if she had been called for to help in some way, to the end of my days I'll wonder who has called her: the ballerina being partnered? J. S. Bach? or, from the depths of his creative energy, Balanchine? And what need is she fulfilling? Perhaps to protest the brutal assault that Denby recognized as an implication of the partnering imagery before the choreographer slowed the tempo? I fantasize, but part of the magic of Balanchine's work is that, despite the choreographer's often-stated disdain for fantasizing projections by onlookers, his ballets invite them. The less narrative material Balanchine put into his dance making, the more seductive it can be to the audience's imagination.

In the last third or so of Balanchine's career, he was often said to aver that abstract ballet didn't exist, because if you put a man and a woman on the stage you have a story. Sometimes, he'd be quoted as adding, "How much story do you want?" But there is evidence that, in fact, he did think abstractly in the making of some of his works—like a chess player or a football coach or an old-school military strategist. To devise the entrance of the seven clans—that is, to get seventy individuals onstage—in the Scottish tattoo that opens *Union Jack* (1976) can only be accomplished through abstract thinking in terms of design and timing. "You invest too much in the individual dancer," Dunham wrote that Balanchine told her when the two were at work on *Cabin in the Sky,* for which he was both director and credited choreographer. "A dancer should be an object for a choreographer. The dancer should not think." There is a wonderful example of how abstract Balanchine's own thinking could get in *Hollywood* (1967), the memoir of screenwriter Garson Kanin, who happened to be present in the late 1930s at a meeting between Balanchine and Samuel Goldwyn. I quote it in full not only because it is a read for the ages but also because it describes a kind of thought pattern that obtains not only for Balanchine but for many choreographers, for poets of the stature of Osip Mandelstam, perhaps for nearly all composers, and—without question—for many visual artists, regardless of whether the art is figurative or abstract:

> "Jesus Christ!" said Goldwyn. "Mr. Balanchine. This ballet you're doing for *The Goldwyn Follies* . . . I know it's great, George." Balanchine shrugged, modestly. Goldwyn went on. "But what's it *about,* Mr. Balanchine?"
>
> "About," said Balanchine.
>
> His assistant sprang to his side and whispered something into his ear.
>
> Balanchine nodded, gravely.
>
> "About," said Balanchine frowning. "Is difficult."
>
> "Never mind," said Goldwyn sternly. "We're all friends here."
>
> Balanchine appeared to retire into himself for a long, troubled

time. We all waited with varying degrees of impatience. My own instinct was that an interior earthquake was about to hit.

Balanchine rose, moved purposefully to Goldwyn's desk, and cleared it. (Would Goldwyn stand for *this?* I wondered. He did.) We all gathered around the desk. It seemed the thing to do.

Balanchine looked about for necessary props, found them. Goldwyn's silver carafe and a large onyx paperweight.

"Difficult," he said, "Because ahb-*strahct,* yes? Two group. Sixteen both. Eight of boy. Eight of girl. First group—positive." He held up the carafe. "Other group—negative." He held up the paperweight. "So. Is four movements of classical form. Suite or sonata. Gershwin knows. We have discuss. So. First movement. Positive." He slammed the carafe down onto the middle of the desk, denting it. Goldwyn, concentrated on the demonstration, took no heed of the damage. Balanchine, a wild look in his eyes, began to move the carafe about, intoning, "Positive. Positive. Positive. Pos-i-tive!" He slid the carafe off the desk and replaced it gently with the paperweight as he cried, "Second movement! Negative!" He moved the paperweight about in a hypnotic pattern. The carafe again. "Third! Positive positive positive." The paperweight. "Negative negative negative."

Fred Kohlmar whispered to me, "Sort of like the old shell game, huh?"

I prayed that Goldwyn had not overheard.

Balanchine went on, his face glistening. The carafe and the paperweight had become living things. The patterns were fascinating and imaginative and surprising.

"Fourth movement!" The action on the desk top went mad. The movements became wilder and wilder.

"Positive negative positive positive negative negative negative positive positive negative negative positive positive positive negative positive positive. Positive. *POS-I-TIVE!*"

He sat, still holding the paperweight, but leaving the carafe in the middle of Goldwyn's desk Goldwyn stared at it. The silence was profound. We all stood stock-still, waiting. Time stood still.

Goldwyn looked up. What did the unreadable expression on his face signify? Pain? Confusion?

"I *like* it!" he said.

On April 24, 2018, the *New York Times* critic Alastair Macaulay published a comment in the paper headlined "Two Seconds That Explain Balanchine." The seconds, also demonstrated in an accompanying Vimeo, were the very opening of *Concerto Barocco*'s first movement, when the women suddenly go from tight fifth position on flat to a tight fifth position on full pointe (the first of the seconds) then, immediately and with full control, drop to an open position with the supporting leg in demi-plié and the working leg pointing behind the body (the second second). Macaulay wants us to recognize as part of Balanchine's creative personality the contrast of tight and open as characteristics—abstract ones, combined with the exactitude of the actions and positions and the speed of them. I disagree with the headline writer that this entirely "explains" Balanchine, yet as Kanin's story makes clear, it does light up a foundational element of Mr. B's dance imagination. Substitute "0" and "1" for his "positive" and "negative," and you have a familiar language from the development of the computer.

A small study might be attempted of the mythic and fairy-tale-like contexts elsewhere in the Balanchine repertory where walking is invested with symbolic or emotional significance, or both. Among them is the procession of Apollo and the Muses in preparation of their ascent to Parnassus at the end of *Apollo*

(1928), the journey of the blinded man and the female "Dark Angel" on his back who intermittently blindfolds him with her hand in the "Elegy" of *Serenade* (1934), the journey of Orpheus and the Dark Angel to the Underworld and the attempt at a return journey to the surface of the earth for Orpheus and Euridice in *Orpheus* (1948), the walking entrance for the princess-ballerina to meet her older male knight in the "Diamonds" section of *Jewels* (1967), the "Walking" pas de deux of 1976 for a ballerina on pointe accompanied by her male partner (affixed to the "Emeralds" section of *Jewels,* where it leads to an image of three gallants kneeling to salute feminine forces who have flown away), and the *Chaconne,* also 1976, set to Christoph Gluck's "happy ending" Paris version of his opera *Orfeo ed Euridice,* which features a pas de deux that takes place, it seems, on a floor of clouds. In the theater, *Chaconne* opens with the "Dance of the Blessed Spirits," a work for nine women with flowing hair, whose careful walking steps in a network configuration become gently elevated into the danced ballet step bourrée, a peregrination on the tips of the toes—a walk for angels. The figures of Orpheus and Euridice walk through this beatific flock, which melts away as the couple approach one another from opposite corners of the stage. However, in the *Dance in America* filming of excerpts from *Chaconne* for PBS, which Balanchine and director Merrill Brockway made in the late 1970s, the couple, Suzanne Farrell and Peter Martins, begin positioned back to back, facing solitary directions, having failed the test of walking, she in his wake, from the Underworld to daylight without validating one another's presence—that is, they have arrived on the surface of the world entirely on the basis of mutual trust. And suddenly, tremorous with uncertainty and expectation, through the miracle of Gluck's music, the dancers pivot to face one another. Once again, Orpheus takes Euridice's hand, he looks into her eyes, and in a journey to mutual bliss, they plunge into a partnership that, as one, walks, swims, and flies.

For each of these works, Balanchine was specific about how, precisely, the dancers should step. For example: Mimi Paul, the ballerina for whom the *Emeralds* "Walking" pas de deux was made, told NYCB dancer Sara Mearns, whom Paul was coaching in the dance for the George Balanchine Video Archives of the Balanchine Foundation: "This is one thing he did say to me: As if you're on a tightrope. Each toe is placed on a line—not a développé but not a stiff walk. The minute the toe touches the floor the other [foot's] toes are coming off to go. A sense of lightness: Try to feel it, not observe it. You've already been walking [that is, imagine what you and your partner have been doing before you appear on the stage]. There's already an atmosphere that's been created." Later that day, in an interview with Nancy Goldner, Mimi Paul said of the pas de deux, "It's like a walking meditation."

New Bach

Robert Garland, the resident choreographer of DTH, made his *New Bach* of 2001 close to 9/11. Although he jokingly calls it "postmodern-urban-neoclassicism," it is, in fact, a classical ballet with the women on pointe, and a homage to Balanchine, specifically, to *Concerto Barocco,* the first ballet that Balanchine gave to DTH for its repertory and a work of classicism that Balanchine rehearsed on at least one occasion with a call to his own NYCB dancers to be "jazzier." Garland's musicality is both sophisticated and witty; his classical movement from time to time incorporates touches of swing or call-and-response phrases, associated with African American gospel song structure, and an especially impressive male solo manages to "speak" in ballet while creating imagery evocative of unchaining, as in its use of unspooling fast, linked, two-footed chaîné turns (*chaîné* in French meaning chain or links). Most characteristic, though, are the passages of walking for the women. In an emailed interview, Garland explained that Arthur Mitchell—the Balanchine star who was, with the teacher Karel Shook, DTH's co-founder—favored a style of theatrical walking that the dancers nicknamed "The Tip":

> It's a distinction between a literal walk and being on one's toes balletically. "Tip. Tip. Tip. Tip" [it goes]. Very musical. It's sort of like a ballet version of Naomi Campbell's impressive runway presence, with that same power. Mr. Mitchell loved Naomi Campbell. [He thought] it didn't suit women of color to be frail. The walk is a very different approach from a vogueing sensibility, which actually deconstructs walking. The D.T.H. "Tip" is about assertion. It allows your hips to respond freely to your gait. Mr. Mitchell would say, "Show the back of your legs!" as you walked— the underneath. It would instantly transform a dancer.

The Long Walk

I saw this dance from 2001 in person only once: its choreographer, David Gordon, and Valda Setterfield, his partner, rarely performed it. But how affecting it was—and how simple. They stood together, side by side and centrally placed, all the way upstage from the audience of the small theater. Nyman's music, thematic, perhaps with a little sob at the heart of it, began to cycle. Gordon placed his arm across Setterfield's shoulders, and the pair began to inch forward as one, swaying ever so slightly as they advanced. It seemed to take a long time, a lifetime one might say. (Valda Setterfield [b. 1934]—Gordon's muse, is also known widely for her years as a cherished dancer with Merce Cunningham and as a dancer and an actor for stage and screen— and David Gordon [1936–2022]—renowned for theatrical works masterminding words, music, and movement in a magical momentum that makes everything seem to be dance—were married for sixty-one years at the time of Gordon's death and are the parents of a son, Ain Gordon, heralded for his own works of performance art.) And yet, although the movement of the walk remained the same from beginning to end, its effect changed as the music's cycles altered and, most of all, as the small figures upstage grew on their journey approaching downstage. By their arrival, I, for one, felt as if I'd lived through a novel by Tolstoy— and was better off as a human being for the experience.

In that emotional effect, *The Long Walk* was not unlike the famous procession of thirty-six ballerinas in white tutus in "The Kingdom of the Shades" scene of Petipa's *La Bayadère,* descending a ramp with the same spectacular step into arabesque allongée, then a weight shift to the back leg, then several small steps forward, then again, over and over and over, as the orchestra repeats a tinkling, Palm Court series of descending scales by Ludwig

Minkus. In the plot, the dancers are spirits wafting through the male protagonist's opium dream. However, the vision has something for everyone: for the first production, in 1877, at the Imperial Theatre of Saint Petersburg, Petipa and his collaborators took the imagery of Solor's vision from one of Gustave Doré's then-well-known and admired illustrations of Dante's *Divine Comedy*, where transparent spirits are shown spiraling through galactic space. So, if you find it discomfiting to, so to speak, lie down with Solor's betrayal of both his true love and the woman who competed with her for his hand, you can comfort your sensibilities with the high art of the reference. (In Petipa's last production, in 1899, the location of the Shades was dropped to a Himalayan mountain pass, although the glorious arabesques remained elevated.)

Gordon himself was fascinated with "The Kingdom of the Shades" scene—fascinated that audiences in opera houses would sit through its repetitions mesmerized. In 1979, as part of a work he called *The Matter (plus and minus)*, to a recording of the Minkus score, he staged a line of regular people in regular daytime clothing who moved horizontally from wing to wing while maintaining a social distance between one another. "I instructed them to stay six feet apart," he told me on the phone in an interview shortly before his death in 2022, "and to step at a place in the music as they joined the queue, and to please stay alive, not become a zombie or a corpse, not look around, do a precise walk that had rules about space and time."

Gordon went on:

The Long Walk: I stay up late, and I can close the huge barn door between our studio and living space and work by myself. I began to work on this walk. All I did was transfer my weight from right side to left side and then to right and then to left and move half a step each time. Things start to gather. I worked and worked on *The Long Walk.* I used Michael Nyman records [to develop the work to], and I detected that I did not speed up or change as Michael Nyman's music did, and that made my miniscule move more dramatic. At some point I needed to show this to somebody: Was it preposterous or obvious? Ain and Valda came into the studio. I put them at one end, and I came toward them. And Ain said, "Keep going!" I wanted Valda with me. It was a *duet;* it was two people walking. We decided how we would do it, from the back to the front. Phil Sandstrom lit it first at Danspace, and, as we moved, the light moved with us. We were taking the light with us as we went, and we were leaving the darkness behind us.

Personal little stories are in the back of everything. When my father was eleven years old, he walked away from school on the Lower East Side, and he started smoking and worked for the rest of his life. When he was in his sixties the three packs a day were killing him and he had to be connected to an oxygen tank. My father is self-conscious and vain and doesn't want to be seen in the street with an oxygen tank. My mother does the grocery shopping. She asks me to go with her, and I do. We walk hand in hand, as she has had cataract surgery and has big glasses. In front of us is an old couple, walking arm and arm. My mother says to me, "I thought that's what I would have with your father."

Gordon concluded: "The complications of life turn out to be the most interesting thing about it. Diana, the princess [of Wales], walking across the minefield is a symbol."

It happens out that, at least in English, there is something of a link between poetry and walking built right into the lingo: a poetic foot, consisting of stressed and unstressed syllables (there are four basic poetic feet), is used to measure the meter of a poem, as a human hand is used to measure the height of a horse. Then there is the word "verse," which has all kinds of meanings in a poetic context—the measurement of a line, a collection of lines that forward the poem's idea or story, and so forth. But the etymology of "verse" is more tactile, more physical. It comes from the Old English "vers," which comes from the Latin "versus," meaning a furrow—that is, the groove made by a plow. The walking farmer plows a furrow and then makes a turning, and that is a verse, in whole or in part. This connection between walking and poetry is baked into the term "volta," used to refer to the way a sonnet's argument makes a turn at the end. And it has been majestically embodied in the vision scene of *La Bayadère,* where, as the Shades exit the ramp, they slowly fill the stage in the pattern of a farmer plowing—first a line (furrow) then a turn, then a line, then another turn. The idea of the scene, with its descent of sacred spirits in moonlit radiance, was inspired by Doré; however, the reversing design in space and the dotted rhythm of their processional walk were among Petipa's monumental accomplishments.

6 battles, without and within

During the pandemic, network TV stations ran an automobile ad that features a little girl, around eight years old, getting into the passenger side of a sedan's front seat after her boxing lesson. Disheartened, she tells the driver—her mother—that the boxing teacher, finding her too much of a ladybugweight for the sport, had suggested she take up dancing instead. In keeping with the car, which goes from mellow to moxie in a nanosecond, her mom is pumped. It takes only a spin around the block for mom to convince daughter to dump dance, don those gloves, and treat the punching bag to a hearty workout. The message for human beings of the female persuasion who aspire to toughen up: You want role models? Forget the bal-lerina beehives and *Papillons* of nineteenth-century Russia; float like a butterfly then sting like a bee at Gold's Gym!

Now, a similar ad for a father and son would pack no punch, because boxing and vernacular dance—specifically, men's rhythm tapping—already go together like rhythm and blues. As the tap-dance historian and performer Jane Goldberg put it in an inter-view published in *Tablet* on December 8, 2008: "Tap, at its red-hot core, is about competition and challenge. Guys younger than Gregory [Hines, who was a good friend of Goldberg's] may not like the challenge mentality, but they still know who the champ is. They like to think that they're as good as Savion [Glover]; and they are all really good. But in that black male tradition—tap and boxing came out of the same era. A couple of tappers from Bubba Gaines's act were also boxers." So, there are two dance flaws in the car ad. One is that the dancing to which the boxing coach suggests the little girl be exiled is implied to be something frilly, anything but rhythm tap, yet the frilly ballet alternative is just as competitive as boxing, if not more. And of course, that the choice between dancing and boxing is specious. In the twenty-first century, aspiring ballerinas can look to both Margot Fon-teyn and Muhammad Ali as role models for self-improvement.

Or Fonteyn and Bruce Lee. An example: in February 2021, *Pointe* magazine staged an online interview with then twenty-three-year-old Sarah-Gabrielle Ryan, who was (and may still be) enjoying featured opportunities as a dancer at Pacific Northwest Ballet, in Seattle. In addition to her technique classes, rehears-als, performances, teaching of others, and wellness practices, her daunting schedule to keep in condition includes two nights a week of martial arts cross-training. What's contemporary about this isn't that girls and women are boxing or even that cross-training is a concept for an athletic endeavor. It's that an aggressive practice would be useful as a cross-training for *dance*.

In 2019, the Metropolitan Museum of Art in New York offered museumgoers a series of dance-based presentations as a way to bring onlookers into the art on exhibit or to showcase the collection by provoking one to think of "then" in the context of "now." One brilliantly conceived program, "Battle! Hip-Hop in Armor," was developed by the museum in tandem with It's Showtime NYC!—an arm of the urban presenting organization Dancing in the Streets, which offers development and performing opportunities to the city's street dancers. The program called attention to the Met's Arms and Armor Department. Over the better part of a year, dancers with the Showtime names of WiildKard, Klassic, and Flexx presented public rehearsals and performances of hip-hop dance battles—one-on-one challenge dances—with the dancers wearing close approximations of armor and chain mail, which the museum had purchased for the program.

At the performance I attended, the capacity audience had more children than adults and more girls than boys. In addition, as I write, on the Met's website is a film of two elementary-school-age reporters from #MetKids who interviewed the dancers. Both are girls of around the age of the girl in the car ad: Karlissah, nine, and Naomi, eleven. They ask just the right questions: What style of dancing do you do? (Klassic: "My main style of dance would be Flexn, which is a reggae dancehall-based style that was created in Brooklyn.") How do you start a dance battle that's similar to olden times? (Wiildkard: "When I'm challenging someone to battle, I'm coming straight towards them. All my focus and my energy's on them, and I'm really trying my best to intimidate them.") When Klassic asks the girl reporters what inspired them to dance, Naomi says that she began in school and that dancing "brought me out of my shell." Karlissah says that what she can take from dancing is "having a wild imagination and just flowing, and . . . dancing to [my] imagination." The helmets and steel gloves with their articulated finger pieces, the padded jackets and chain mail that shadowed the body's actions, the arms and armor of the Middle Ages and the Renaissance, so formidably authoritarian and unknowable in the museums of my own childhood, had become *interesting* and *knowable* from the inside—at least for the moment—to these little girls, these dancing reporters from a dawning generation.

In the case of European warfare, from at least the Renaissance onward, the horses of warriors—their heads and bodies encased in armor—were, like their riders, rigorously conditioned for battle. In the horses' case, that was accomplished through a group of exacting maneuvers that have become the competitive art of dressage, and such centers of equine deportment as the Spanish Riding School in Vienna continue to train talented steeds (Lipizzaners, in this case) to study that challenging art at its most elevated level of mastery. Some of the imagery and vocabulary are clearly connected to ballet, although whether through a cause-and-effect relationship or a parallel evolution isn't certain. When the horse choreography is coordinated with music, so that the footfalls of the horses in their various gaits are matched to certain notes or chords in rhythmic patterns, the timekeeping effect is of dance, and there are separate competitions just for that terpsichorean effect. (Once, at a Long Island demonstration of this almost unbelievable skill on the part of animal and human rider working in concert, I reported on a dancing horse named Genius, Mozart a specialty.) The more difficult maneuvers include the pirouette (the horse rises on its back legs, its forelegs tucked up, and then, step by dainty step, traces a complete circle in place before returning to earth), the capriole (the horse jumps and simultaneously kicks both pairs of legs outward, like a goat), and the courbette (the horse hops forward on its back legs alone, its forelegs tucked up, so that the two back legs, in practical terms, become one, giving the effect of a ballerina hopping on the pointe of one foot).

In a reciprocal exchange, the lexicon of ballet has a "horse step" (pas de cheval), which re-creates the image of a horse pawing on the ground. As with the practice of classical ballet, the animals that are selected to perform these actions in public are chosen to be trained for their bodies and their temperaments. Strength and reliability mattered in war. As in ballet, optics also matters in dressage. A spring 2021 virtual seminar, in Paris, on "Horse Ballet of the 17th and 18th Centuries" attracted some of the leading scholars and practitioners of equine art; it was there I learned that the conventional explanation of how those dressage maneuvers originated—to clear a protective space around the rider in battle is what I was taught—is now considered incorrect, the explanation being that such a practice would have exposed the animal's belly, its most vulnerable (and, in war, unarmored) body part.

From ancient times, around the world, dancing has been part of culture, not only as an expression of joy and triumph but as a construction to address the mystery of Creation, to pay homage to the natural world as represented by the animals that humans hunted to eat, to carry the history of a people through time via steps and gestures, to test the mettle of warriors and of adolescents coming of age, to implore assistance from universal forces of healing, and—most theatrically—to mimic and, thereby, to effect symbolically, the otherwise unnatural transformations that result from humankind's profound yet inexplicable ability to pick up a willow switch and envision it as a magic wand. That visionary dimension is one dimension of dance.

Yet there is a realistic dimension as well. In that, the performer embodies—takes on—the spirit of the subject of the dance; the elements of that spirit, translated into the dancer's movements, are based upon close observation of the subject in the wild. Dancing, in this sense, might be thought of as a naturalist's notes. African cultures have produced solos, for example, in which the dancer "dances" (becomes) various kinds of birds. From Latin America to Asia, dancers have embodied the sacred deer, although emphasizing very different aspects of the animal—its exhilarating leaps in the theaters of Mexico, its meditative stillnesses in the Cham version of Tibet. Among Native Americans and Canadian First Peoples, dances have embodied the dreams and visions of the community reenacted physically, sometimes with rich imaginative imagery, such as the spectacles (including horseback choreography) described by Black Elk in several of his twentieth-century oral histories. All of these dances are driven by stories, sometimes quite simple and sometimes elaborate.

One finds very ancient connections, indeed, in human civilization not only between dance and music but also between dance and narrative or dramatic poetry. The great epics of India—the Ramayana and the Mahabharata—are celebrated by India's own quite distinct Hindu and Muslim classic dance traditions, as well as by the court dances and storytelling puppetry of, variously, Cambodia (where there is also a tradition of dancing kings), Thailand, and, with seemingly unending variety, Indonesia. There are the folk dance-dramas for the water puppets of Vietnam and Laos, once performed inside rice paddies, with the water itself as the stage. In the legacy dance and theater traditions of Japan, Formosa (now Taiwan), Korea, Bhutan, China, there is much more to contemplate—about the negotiations between dancing and poetry, the identities of sacred and secular performance, the nuances of meaning achieved by rigorously disciplined technique, and the way nonperforming audiences are trained by the performers to recognize all of these. For, although art forms tend to be maintained by their executants, even under duress or having suffered the loss of the world in which the forms were engendered, maintenance alone will not make the art thrive, much less flourish. That requires an audience, aware of what is being "said" and, as important, implied through movement and physical touches alone, and whose need to be in the presence of those statements at regular intervals gives them energizing urgency and educates the next generation.

A point worthy of pondering is articulated by Joseph Houseal, the director of the Chicago-based organization Core of Culture ("Dedicated to safeguarding intangible world culture and assisting the continuity of ancient dance traditions and embodied spiritual practices where they originate, and beyond") in his column of May 15, 2021, for the online magazine *Buddhistdoor Global:* "One main distinction between Eastern and Western dancing is that Eastern traditions, particularly sacred ones, have a fully developed inner technique that corresponds to external body movement. Western dances don't." The key word, I believe, is "technique." A Western dancer's unspoken thoughts or meditations may be projected simultaneously in performance by external body movement, as in the dance traditions of Asia, but there is no communal procedure, polished over centuries, for the Western dancer to make the projection of interior life reliably parallel to the movement. (During this century, dance as a field has become at least as invested in mind-body practices for wellness as for training.)

Still, regardless of whether one is speaking of Eastern or Western dance traditions, movement alone is not enough for a dance work to be convincingly called art. There has to be a level of feeling, imagery, meaning, mission that is everywhere present and nowhere visible by which the movement is motivated. Steps and gestures can more or less come and go without the work losing its core identity, but if that interior level of cohesion is damaged, then choreography ceases to exist as an art work and becomes exercise—as, for instance, with Gagaku, the ancient Japanese warrior dance tradition, once exclusively performed for the emperor but, in our era, simply one more regimen that women as well as men can call upon to stay in shape through weekly classes, like pole dancing.

I used to think that if choreographers would just try to share their own thoughts, unbidden fantasies, and deliberate meditations—disclose that interior—then dancing would be easy to understand. Today, I'm of the opposite persuasion. For that interior core level, consisting of flying associations among unrelated or irrationally related memories and narratives, can be misconstrued and framed as literal craziness, something permanently dangerous instead of psychic energy tutored and harnessed in service of aesthetics rather than ethics. Artists themselves become sensitive to how their contemporaries might regard them, with self-censorship as a result—commercial wisdom in the short run yet, perhaps, a loss in the long. An example is the following edited excerpt from Balanchine's dialogue with the poet-journalist-musician Jonathan Cott concerning the choreographer's two-act ballet *A Midsummer Night's Dream* (1962), first published in Cott's interview with Balanchine for *Rolling Stone* magazine in 1978 and republished in Lincoln Kirstein's *Portrait of Mr. B* in 1984.

[Balanchine, quoting the play:] When Bottom the Weaver is transformed into an ass, he says: "The eye of man hath not heard, the ear of man hath not seen, man's hand is not able to taste, his tongue to conceive, nor his heart to report what my dream was." It sounds silly, but it's full of double and triple meanings. And I think that at moments like this, Shakespeare was a Sufi. It reminds me of St. Paul's First Epistle to the Corinthians [1 Corinthians 2, 9]: "Eye hath not seen, nor ear heard, neither have entered into the heart of man the things that God hath prepared for them that love him." What Bottom says sounds as if the parts of the body were quarreling with each other. But it's really as if he were somewhere in the Real World. He loses his man's head and brain and experiences a revelation.

And then what happens? Bottom wants to recite his dream "which hath no bottom," to the Duke after his and his friends' play-within-a-play is over, but the Duke chases them away. And the really deep and important message was in that dream.

At one point, when I was choreographing the ballet, I said to myself: In the last act, I'll make a little entertainment and then a big vision of Mary, standing on the sun, wrapped in the moon, with a crown of twelve stars on her head and a red dragon with seven heads and ten horns . . . the Revelation of St. John!

Why didn't you do it?

Well, because then I thought that nobody would understand it, that people would think I was an idiot.

"The lunatic, the lover, and the poet / Are of imagination all compact," Shakespeare says elsewhere in the play.

That's it. I knew it was impossible. I wished I could have done it. But instead, in the second act, I made a pretty—not silly or comic—pas de deux to a movement from an early Mendelssohn string symphony [*Symphony No. 9 in C*]—something people could enjoy.

One Balanchine dancer who not only believed in Balanchine's *Midsummer* vision—which the choreographer had wrestled with in himself and abandoned—but had gone so far as to put a bit of it on the stage was Francia Russell, a member of the original cast of his masterpiece *Agon* (1957). Russell danced for Balanchine from 1956 to 1961, when she retired from NYCB as a soloist. For a year, she performed for Jerome Robbins in his Ballets: USA, then for two years she taught at the School of American Ballet, and then, in 1964, when she was in her mid-twenties, Balanchine appointed her a ballet master of the company and, for the rest of his life, sent her around the world to stage his works. So far, she has overseen some 125 stagings throughout the United States, Europe, and Asia. In the late 1970s, Russell and her husband, the choreographer Kent Stowell—also an NYCB alumnus—became co-artistic directors of Pacific Northwest Ballet, in Seattle, serving until 2005. (Russell also directed the company school, now named for her.) When, in 1997, Russell and Stowell asked designer Martin Pakledinaz to redesign PNB's entire production of *Midsummer,* which had been in the company's repertory since 1985, they discussed Balanchine's comments to Cott with the designer. Although the team decided that the choreographer's vision of the Apocalypse, delivered full strength, wasn't right for PNB's audiences any more than for NYCB's, Pakledinaz indicated a clue to the imagery in his night sky backdrop for the second-act divertissement, which takes place outdoors under a huge crescent moon, a synecdoche for the "big vision of Mary" and the dragon—evoked for those with eyes to see it. To my knowledge, this production is the sole staging of the ballet with even the slightest acknowledgment of what Balanchine told Cott he understood Shakespeare's play really to be about.

Of course, dancing still matters when it isn't intended as art. For much of this century, a heralded dance program for patients with

Parkinson's has been offered by the Mark Morris Dance Group, in Brooklyn, and similar programs have been developed at dance centers around the world. Directed by the virtuoso Mark Morris company dancer David Leventhal, founding teacher of the program, Dance for PD has been endorsed by the American Parkinson Disease Association, whose website contains a film of a class and an interview with Leventhal. Some members of the class sit in chairs or wheelchairs; all participate as fully as they can in the movement—a kind of gestural modern dance. Furthermore, programs around the United States use dance—sometimes in combination with verbal therapies—to treat sufferers from PTSD, especially traumatized refugees who have been subjected to physical assaults and severe bodily indignities. These patients are generally not professional dancers, though. Professional practitioners of exacting dance languages might need a different kind of therapy; they know too much about the way dance works on the body to be able to let go of the authority their knowledge conveys to them. And without surrender, healing cannot begin.

Few dancers in history were more traumatized than those in the court ballet of Cambodia during the reign of Pol Pot, in the 1970s, when, it is estimated, upward of three-quarters of the royal dancers and their musicians were slaughtered and the rest were driven into exile or threatened with the Killing Fields. And yet, again and again, the accounts of survivors able to return to teaching demonstrate an uncompromising approach to the fantastical exactitude of the court dance technique. If your character is fainting, that is not the same as dropping dead, and you must know how to produce the difference right now! If you're asked what you think of an exhibition of Auguste Rodin's celebrated pencil-and-gouache impressions of Cambodian dancers created in 1906, you note that they're beautiful and have the right energy but that the position of that arm is too high. The great artist got many things right, but great or not, he also got that arm position wrong. From the dancer's point of view, finding fault of this type is homage to what was lost. (Of course, life being life, it can also be argued that, in butchering the dancers almost immediately, the Khmer Rouge was enunciating its own perverse version of the statement that dance matters.)

Rodin, though, was usually after something more in his sculptures than anatomical correctness, and it is likely that by making the position of the arm wrong as anatomical reporting he wanted to make it right as drawing. A collector of photographs (and an original subscriber to Eadweard Muybridge's *Animal Locomotion* in 1887), the sculptor was keenly aware of the difference between the facts and what he called the truth (and I'd call the effects) of movement. In his bronze *Saint John the Baptist* of 1877, a figure of a naked man striding, Rodin counterintuitively achieved the impression of forward movement by representing the figure's legs with each foot fully on the ground while the torso is oriented in such a way that the body's weight seems to be in the process of being transferred onto the front leg. "Take my St. John, for example," Rodin said, in conversation with writer Paul Gsell in *Rodin on Art and Artists* (translated into English by Katharine Waldo Douglas under the byline Mrs. Romilly Fedden and published in 1957). "While he is represented with both feet on the ground, a snapshot of a model executing the same movement would probably show the back foot already raised and moving in the direction of the other one." The *Saint John the Baptist* sculpture was partially used as the basis for Rodin's headless and armless figure of 1907, *The Walking Man;* this, too, presents both feet on the ground, although the back leg is tweaked, slightly turned out, and the torso is slightly reoriented from their earlier counterparts. Rodin knew what he wanted: not the fact of the transfer of weight in a stride but rather the moment of transformation, the before-and-after of a step represented simultaneously. (Alberto Giacometti's celebrated *Walking Man* or *Striding Man* bronzes of 1961 show the anatomically correct, explicitly lifted heel of the back foot as meticulously as Rodin avoided showing it.)

Later in his life, in the years of the twentieth century before World War I, Rodin became fascinated by dancers, and he sculpted as well as drew them. His sketching session in a public garden with the Royal Cambodian Ballet was photographed as news. In contrast, he kept from any public exhibition his quickly made sculptural impressions, in clay, of a naked model in extreme positions, which he could deconstruct and use to experiment in unconventional recombinations. Regardless of whether the situation was public or private, though, he was not making art to illustrate the physical facts of his subjects, as independent measurement might validate his reporting. Nor was he tracking the subjectivity of his perceptions of the dancers in space. As he told Gsell, he was, instead, reaching through the body to the soul, a gesture different for every figure. In his unique sculpture of Vaslav Nijinsky, probably from a stage memory, Rodin grasped a small mammalian intelligence hunched over one knee, the other leg extended with a blunt force, every part of his person driven not by beauty but by vitality, perhaps in air. (Nijinsky felt, after visiting Rodin once, that the artist found his short, powerfully muscled body poorly put together, unaesthetic, although Rodin did make a few nude drawings of him. It is not clear whether Nijinsky saw the sculpture.)

How different that Nijinsky soul is from the one Rodin discovered in many quick drawings of the face and body of a preferred model, Japanese actress-dancer Hanako ("Little Flower," the stage name of Ōhta Hisa, a dancer presented to the Parisian public by Loïe Fuller, one of Rodin's admirers). However, what these works about dancers do share is the sculptor's magical trapping of their physical energy, whether, as with the Nijinsky piece, in three dimensions, or, as in the pictures on paper of Hanako, in two. Instead of working from the surface of the body at any given instant to the spiritual depth of the goal toward which the body aims, Rodin proceeds in reverse, from the depth of the interior journey to enlightenment regarding the appearance of the bodily surface. The artist's restless pilgrimage from the interior origin of expressiveness in a subject to its visible projection, without punctilious concern for what might be the rules and regulations governing what pose is taken—proprieties independent of *how* it is taken—is one of the distinctions between the sculptures and drawings of Rodin and the ballet art works by Edgar Degas. For Degas, regardless of the model's nudity, her arabesque allongée is eternally an arabesque allongée, and the stance of the relaxed balletic fourth position taken by *Little Dancer Aged Fourteen* is unmistakably fourth position, not first or third. (Pierre

Renoir's own earlier painting of a ballet girl, *The Dancer,* shows the actress Henriette Hanriot—who was actually fourteen years old when she modeled for that painting—in a tight fifth position. Emotionally, the significant difference between Renoir's dancer and all the dancers of Degas is that Renoir's looks directly and powerfully at the painter-viewer, while Degas's dancers either look in their own chosen direction or, as with his *Little Dancer,* whose gaze is hooded, look downward. Rodin's dancers barely have faces or even heads; the emotion of those works, entirely sited in their bodies, is not something the dancer feels—only what the artist sees.)

Sometimes, Rodin's work shows the energy of the figures to be linked to erotic themes, as in the scores of small clay statues, known as *Mouvements de danse,* which were derived from the posing of Alda Merano, a petite acrobatic dancer at the Opéra Comique, who had a proud Spanish back and a considerable flexibility in her joints countered by resilience and strength. She could take an attitude (a bent-legged pose) to the back and reach both her arms overhead and behind her to seize the toe of the raised foot and pull it toward her head, thereby closing a circle that turned her figure into an abstraction while revealing or making accessible her genitalia. The pose has been practiced by acrobats, clothed as well as unclothed, since time immemorial, but to see it realized by a flesh-and-blood young woman who is entirely naked—as Merano was while demonstrating for the camera in a turn-of-the-twentieth-century photograph—might give even a roué pause. In that circa 1905 magazine photograph of the acrobat, sultry and bobbed-haired, Merano uses her right hand alone to seize her uplifted toe behind her. Meanwhile, the little finger of her left hand, held out at waist height, springs up and arches forward suggestively, almost as if the digit were separately alive. The pose, notated as "Dance Movement A," is, as Merano demonstrates it, not merely an action used to limber up but rather a curated presentation, a species of performance. Rodin drew Merano and sculpted her in two ways: using one hand to catch her foot behind her while her free hand gestured, as in the photo, and using two hands to catch her toe behind her, which brings forward the pose's implicit geometry and causes the model's personality to recede. (In discussing Rodin here, I am indebted to *Rodin on Art and Artists,* the artist's translated conversations with Paul Gsell, and the meticulously conceived and realized catalog to the Courtauld Gallery show *Rodin and Dance: The Essence of Movement,* edited by Alexandra Gerstein—especially the key paragraph included from the hallmark essay on Rodin written in 1962 by the art critic and historian Leo Steinberg.)

Not only many artists but also choreographers have joined Rodin's search for souls in the acrobatic catching of the toe (and foot sole) by a performer reaching heavenward and then, as into time past, behind herself. Prominent in ballet history is the *Tanzsynfonia*'s Fyodor Lopukhov, one of the leading Russian ballet experimentalists of the early USSR, who introduced the same erotic-abstract pose that had magnetized Rodin into a spectacularly acrobatic pas de deux he choreographed for his ballet *The Ice Maiden* (1929), based on Hans Christian Andersen's novella. In Andersen's story, Art is embodied as a goddess, cold and uncaring of everything except her ravenous need. She lives in a glacier in the Alps and claims the artist from his human bride through a glacial kiss. During the pas de deux, the ballerina, costumed in a unitard "skin," reaches back with both hands to catch the toe of one foot while standing on pointe with the other—and then her partner revolves her in place 360 degrees, thereby turning her into a life-sized architectural element; as in Andersen's story, she is transformed into classical art before our eyes. How different in its tender humanity is Balanchine's use of the pose in the pas de deux from *Agon,* where the man, introducing the idea of catching her leg behind her to the ballerina, reaches back to help her catch her leg as she stands on pointe. Then she shows him she is able to do the catch on her own, and he drops to the floor, supine with wonder, as if her soul has just been revealed to him. For several preceding decades, Balanchine himself had been obsessed with the theme of Andersen's Ice Maiden, yet he was never able to perfect the production of the story that he dreamed of. Sometimes, in watching the *Agon* pas de deux, I wonder if, among many things it achieves, it realizes the triumphant marriage of the Ice Maiden and the Poet she claims, who teaches her how to accomplish something new.

For many choreographers, dancing is the ligature between poses or still points. Whether calmly or explosively, it connects. Now, consider another possibility: the dance as intangible momentum that—through a kind of jump-cut editing—comprises only the still moments themselves. You have the late-life choreographic experiments of Merce Cunningham, using the software programs

LifeForms and DanceForms as collaborators to generate movement. The dance writer and publicist Ellen Jacobs explained the process definitively in a *New York Times* article on Cunningham and computers on September 1, 2020.

> With its graphic division of the body into three regions—legs, head/torso and arms—LifeForms allowed Cunningham to disrupt the natural chain of joint action. Imagine extending your arm, then instead of allowing the natural follow through, which would be a linear stretch of the wrist and hand, you bent the wrist downward, and stuck out your thumb. If an avatar could challenge natural expectations and shoot its arm forward with wrist bent and thumb stuck outward, then why couldn't a dancer?

Two solos, especially, that Cunningham made with the computer for members of his company were hair-raising to see live in the theater and can still be perused on YouTube: one was made for Holley Farmer in the dance *Loose Time,* from 2002 ("It felt like a rapid series of different thunderbolts, from one part of the body after another; and what made it exciting was that the remainder of Ms. Farmer's body always stayed braced, never reacting to the explosion," the critic Alastair Macaulay wrote in "The Body's War Within: Stillness Versus Motion" in the *New York Times* on December 29, 2008), and the other, originally made for Jonah Bokaer in *Split Sides* (2003), was learned by Silas Reiner in 2011 and performed so well that one could hardly believe what one was seeing—jumps, for instance, that took off from nowhere. In each of the two dances, every moment is, paradoxically, both a poised moment and a continuity. "I think drama is contrast," Cunningham told Nancy Dalva, Merce Cunningham

Trust Scholar in Residence, during an interview on July 30, 2008 (still unpublished), for the online series *Mondays with Merce*. He added that he didn't employ specific dramas in his choreography but that his use of chance operations to determine sequences could make the contrast between before and after a given moment so strong that "one has to figure out how to *do* that," and the story of the solution becomes the story of the work.

From *Chance and Circumstance* (2009), the remarkable memoir by Carolyn Brown of dancing for Cunningham and John Cage during the first twenty years of their enterprise, and from other scholarship, it has become clear that Cunningham's dances are full of the choreographer's personal stories and story fragments, none of which are spelled out. They are also full of risk-taking explorations of form, late-life adventures in artistic experiment for its own sake, like Rodin's *Mouvements de danse*.

The virtuosity exemplified in these Cunningham solos is not only a landmark of modern dance but also a treasure of American culture in general. They make the case for why dance matters just by being performed. However, it is also heartening to remember that dancing on a much more basic level—dancing of any style or tradition, performed with correct placement of bones and tendons—serves not only as art and, given the joy it can inspire, as consolation for the body's inadequacies but also as a kind of therapy to improve and strengthen us today for our daily challenges tomorrow. Tango, a stalking dance, has been shown to help with issues of balance. Hip-hop has been shown to help decrease anxiety. The history of classical dance teems with individuals, including some prominent stars, who took up ballet as children in order to address orthopedic problems such as scoliosis and weakness of the feet. And the efficacy of dance goes beyond the healing of frailties to the improvement of the status quo. By many accounts, the greatest Soviet hockey team of all time, under the tough yet innovative twentieth-century coach Anatoly Tarasov, was strengthened by the deep-muscle conditioning afforded to them through their regular study of ballet—specifically of Vaganova training (as was taught over much of the Soviet century to dancers of the Kirov Ballet), bolstered by the coordination afforded from Russian ballet's techniques of character dancing.

Studies are available. For example, the online ResearchGate version of Markham Heid's article, "Why Dancing Is the Best Thing You Can Do for Your Body" (originally appearing in *Time,* July 5, 2017), handily contains cyberlinks to a clutch of scientific papers in peer-reviewed journals. For a deeper dive into neurology, physiology, and anthropology, there is Judith Lynne Hanna's remarkable (and heavily footnoted) book-length explanation of how the knee bone is connected to neuroscience, *Dancing to Learn: The Brain's Cognition, Emotion, and Movement* (2015). Despite the widely accepted thesis that modern humans emerged in Africa nearly two hundred thousand years ago, Hanna proposes as a starting point for the history of dance—that is, the story of dance as a sustained and self-sufficient set of cultural actions, something more than impulsive or ineluctable rhythmic responses to external phenomena, beginning in the womb—a more recent time (some forty thousand years ago) and more northern clime (Europe, during the Upper Paleolithic Age). Her evidence: images in wall paintings and other surviving visual art and the discoveries of (presumably carbon-dated) musical instruments from that period. This is not to say that dance unquestionably originated in that place and moment but rather that the *history* of dance we have—the narrative based on evidence—begins there and then. Wooden dancing masks and dancing sticks, important to African cultures, for example, would not last long enough to testify. Since Hanna's book was published, Paleolithic cave paintings of warty hogs have been discovered in Indonesia. Is it possible that dance, too, developed at once around the globe? Is the mating display of males a universal biological reason why all humans—and some animals—dance?

Early in humanity's history, Hanna writes, dance functioned as a nonverbal, often symbolic language that made it possible for individuals to bond with a social group. As it happens, her thought has been theatrically realized halfway across the world in *Dantza,* the magnificent, feature-length, all-dancing Basque film of 2018. It opens back in the mists of time on a half-naked, hardscrabbling tribe of hairy bipedalists rudely harnessing their animal energies to invent agriculture in an unforgiving terrain. Something happens to their rough walk (shoes, perhaps?), and from movement for the purpose of quelling their visceral hunger they are ineluctably triggered in scene after scene—the hours of the day and the passing seasons providing nature's extratheatrical set—to adopt rites and rhythmic processions on behalf of unseen forces. They evolve through stages of collective epiphany and suffering, transforming gradually from tribes to clans to assemblies of individuals with private interior lives, unique consciousness of the world around them, and multifarious levels of communication. Accompanying their changes in mentality from herd to word is their increasing capacity for individual rhythmic expression, what many readers would consider dancing. By the end of this epic time-travelogue of a movie, the prehistoric populace has become a domesticated culture at a village wedding, the celebrants having continually renegotiated their relationship to nature through dancing, music, mysterious and sometimes gripping enactments, and theatrical transformations. As their physical abilities grow more nuanced, their interior lives—represented by the development of friendships and romantic couplings—become more complex, too, as do the by-products of increasing sophistication in art, architecture, gardening, and technology. Their evolving industry on behalf of the tribe has gentled the landscape and cultivated civil society according to complicated rules of engagement, to the point where the ultimate demonstration of a dancer's joy is the ability to caper and cut the musical meters in soft shoes on top of a half-filled drinking glass. And during the lofting and landing of the dancing body in the course of syncopated jumps on the rim of the tumbler, the liquid remains undisturbed.

Dantza is almost unknown in the United States, alas. According to its online press book, the director, Telmo Esnal, was himself a dancer, and he built the concept for the film over many years with the anthropologist-choreographer Juan Antonio Urbeltz. The inspiration for the Felliniesque look of the film's production design is attributed to the award-winning sculptor Koldobika Jauregi, whose fabulous imagination rings delicate optical changes among forms that seem freshly plucked from the dreams of an anxious child and purifying imagery derived from folklore. This elaborate construction of human evolution as a world of art, centrally represented by dance—sometimes urbane and benign, sometimes savage as a Goya disaster—makes for a mesmerizing couple of hours. After reading about it, I found it on YouTube, where I returned to watch it until suddenly it was taken down, its unpredictable access in keeping with the butterfly-for-a-day character so often (and so often aptly) attributed to dancing in general.

I wonder what an eight-year-old aspiring boxer might think of *Dantza*. What about a boxer-dancer manqué who is eighty going-on-eight? A case in point: the choreographer Twyla Tharp's most recent book, *Keep It Moving: Lessons for the Rest of Your Life* (2019). Tharp, who is partial to boxing as a practice (and whose imagery she has used in some of her dances), writes of the aging body with the appetite of an A+ student sailing through an end-of-term exam. She suggests quite a few physical initiatives to keep that body in tune, including walking, which she took up with rehabilitative fervor after surgery—and, an avid reader, in consultation with the prose of Henry David Thoreau and Marcel Proust. Her goad to her own readers to maintain physical health is bursting with literary inspiration. Proust, for instance, is glimpsed as he places one foot on a stair, as if about to climb it, and then, rocking his weight from front foot to back foot, undergoes a revelation concerning past and future. Tharp's multidirectionality notwithstanding, dancing permeates her book, not only in terms of the motivation and discipline she advises but also in terms of its author's pervasive consciousness of being—in the phrase that Mabel Ellsworth Todd coined to describe the relationship between human physiology and psychology—a "thinking body." Tharp's neuroplasticity in her ninth decade is, so far, clearly unconcussed.

Celebration, war, etiquette, unregulated emotion, the embodiment of a people's unwritten history, the public demonstration of physical beauty as political power (the perfected dancing of the teenaged Louis XIV, the Sun King; the crushingly slow flexions of the goddess apsaras for the Cambodian court); the astronomical insights of spiritual vision, embodied by the whirling planets and celebrated in poems and philosophical tracts from the early Renaissance, the Enlightenment, the writings of Friedrich Nietzsche and Søren Kierkegaard, Ezra Pound, T. S. Eliot, Marianne Moore, Kenneth Koch, Langston Hughes, Joy Harjo: innumerable are the contexts and purposes for dancing across time and place. But fundamental to why dancing as a cultural practice persisted over the past forty thousand years or so is surely, at least in part, the pleasure of doing it. A vivid articulation of that delight was given on a 2021 Dance/NYC symposium panel by Michael Manswell, teacher and artistic director of the vibrant New York City performing company Something Positive ("dedicated to preserving the art and culture of the African diaspora, and its cross-cultural influences"). Asked by the moderator, Rodney Lopez, what his first dance memory was "and how did it make you feel?" Manswell took a long moment to reflect, then, in his richly melodic voice, spoke of himself as a small child: "on my grandmother's steps." He continued:

> My aunt loved Otis Redding . . . we were living in Trinidad, and she would play the same thing over and over, until one day she played Chubby Checker, "Let's Do the Twist!" And I started moving. And of course, Trinidadians are known for the looseness in the pelvis, . . . that whole African thing, whining and carrying on. And I just thought it was *perfect*. It was lovely! And I twisted and twisted and twisted. And I realized even in that, what I would call infantile experience, JOY! The idea that one can be transformed by hearing music and lyrics used in conjunction or in concert with each other that spurts the body into action.

The surging joy that Manswell invoked at the "Streets, Dance Halls, and Living Rooms" panel is almost invariably awoken by dance movement at a lively tempo, what dancers sometimes refer to as "dancey dances," and it can be roused proprioceptively (by physical empathy) in the spectator as well as the performer. I, for one, have experienced it while watching performances as different as a miners' gumboot dance in a 1970s production of the Zulu *Macbeth;* the foamingly fast Cuban maypole dance that Ballet Folklorico Cutumba uncorked at the Brooklyn Academy of Music during the 2011 edition of DanceAfrica; and—every time, with every Royal Danish Ballet cast—in the tarantella that closes August Bournonville's three-act ballet *Napoli* (1842), where the playful, fast-footed variations for dancing couples (which Bournonville wrote to his wife that he built partially on tarantella figures he found in Gaetano Dura's book of 1836 on that dance) erupt in an exhibition of heel-toe joy to which one simply succumbs. (When I say "every," I mean even the exuberant silent film of Bournonville's *Napoli* tarantella made by Peter Elfelt in 1903, with a modern piano subbing for the orchestra in H. S. Paulli's irresistible music. In this film, a vest-pocket version of the stage events, the variations are not distributed among several couples, as in the ballet, but rather are danced for Elfelt's camera entirely by the Royal Danish Ballet legends Valborg Borchsenius and Hans Beck, who achieve their infectiously flirtatious, step-driven advances and retreats in a studio smaller than many of today's closets.)

My own joy in watching this kind of allegro dance figure is not the product of the particular dance tradition exemplified or of the feats of the dancers per se: it arises from the inexplicable effect of the choreography seeming, by way of the spirited response to the music, to free the genius loci of the dancing space. Dancers and audiences connect through waves of reciprocal energy, thereby giving those of us who are open to it the wonderful sense that we all are participating in a phenomenon larger than any one of us.

An example is *Push Comes to Shove,* Twyla Tharp's bravura showcase, made on and for Mikhail Baryshnikov with American Ballet Theatre, in 1976. A practiced magician of choreographic effects, Tharp built up audience suspense about the star—at that time, touted for his peerless classical technique and leaps and recent defection from the Kirov Ballet and the USSR—by introducing him before the closed curtain, as close as he could be to the audience and remain on the opera house stage, in a softly rakish number with a couple of ballerinas joining him for a game of pass-the-hat, to Joseph Lamb's intimate and intimating "Bohemia Rag." Baryshnikov's derby was worn low over his downward-cast eyes, as in Walker Evans's amusingly gangsterish portrait of the young Lincoln Kirstein. Then the trio disappeared behind the curtain, which then itself disappeared. And as the orchestra in Joseph Haydn's "The Bear" symphony proclaimed the next sprightly tune, Baryshnikov catapulted himself through a master craftswoman's enlarged and repunctuated ballet versions of the tightly held, miniaturized off-balance choreography from the rag. The constricted limbs and strict plumb lines in Baryshnikov's precurtain dance posture opened, with the Haydn, into a dancing body speeding in flight, a swinging pendulum. The dance phrases, packed with swooping, full-body slashes through the air and invisible preparations for them on the ground, rolled through the music until crashing into this or that chord; one could almost hear the winning crackle of a bowling ball scattering ten pins. Suddenly, Baryshnikov had slowed down, as if he were in a rehearsal, to palm the sweat from his hair—a moment that anyone in the house could do. And then he was airborne, once more a god. The audiences at the performances I attended—and the reports of other audiences who saw *Push* on tour that first season—could barely contain their joy, or perhaps the word is jubilation.

The late critic David Daniel used to opine that, although ballet could end one day, since it had a fixed beginning (Balthasar de Beaujoyeulx's *Balet comique de la royne,* of 1581), dance was eternal. I write after a year that has suggested otherwise. Staying in place, quarantined, locked down, alone outdoors, podded up, dancers were dancing virtually, masked, socially distanced, and relating to one another in locations far-flung across the world;

for the most part, though, they were doing it while making what are essentially dance films. Encountered through screens, they and we, their audiences, didn't share space—or the waves of reciprocal energy that animate it. Our pandemic world then was provided with plenty of dance imagery but, for the most part, not the felt experience of dancing. The experience of watching dance had become visual, cerebral, mediated, and increasingly obligatory if not exhausting.

In speaking with friends and colleagues, too, I learned that a concern with this element of community, of shared space, is largely generational: if you were born between the world wars or in the twenty years following World War II, a dancer's presence or lack of it in a performance matters very much. Born later (say, from around the Vietnam War forward), presence matters, yet film is also of interest. Familiarity with life experience filtered by screens may be one explanation for the difference. There are more. When I grew up, the song from the Roaring Twenties "The Best Things in Life Are Free" could be taken literally. According to the lyrics by Buddy DeSylva and Lew Brown, the moon, spring flowers, and singing birds are public property. The song doesn't put it that way, of course. Owing to the expensive permissions fees for publishing even one line from a song, I can't give you the actual wording, which is much catchier than my paraphrase. So this happy-go-lucky number has turned out not to be among the best things in life after all, which is apt, since what it says about our birthright as living beings is no longer the case, beginning with the moon, and continuing to elements the song doesn't mention but that it invokes: the air, the water, the forests, the prairies, the wind, the seas, and most of everything else that constitute what we'd call the earth. These are being staked out, for the most part, by nations, although, with private space missions going forward, dibs by private corporations are surely on the way. Furthermore, so many elements of the natural world are imperiled that by the time the earth gets to the twenty-second century, they may not be worth owning, at least in their analog form.

And now, a transcript of a small podcast from our sponsor.

Hey, Girl Reporter here! Pronouns she/her/hers. I am standing on the streetcorner of Now and Forever with Jof and Mia, a young couple just walking out of an Ingmar Bergman retrospective. I understand they'll be tested on it in class tomorrow.

GIRL REPORTER: Jof, what do you think of Bergman's medieval allegory of the Cold War nuclear arms race, *The Seventh Seal*? Does it connect to your life today?

JOF: Sorry. Looking for my Uber. What did you say?

GR: I'm asking you your takeaway from the movie. (Jof disappears into his phone.)

GR: Mia?

MIA: Dead dudes dance up a storm?

GR: Well, I was hoping for something a little more personal. The first time I saw it, in the late sixties, when I was about your age, my entire associations with it were with the violence then rocking my world: assassinations at home, the Vietnam War and Agent Orange abroad; Bobby Seale gagged and shackled in the courtroom; the best minds of my generation strung out to dry on drugs. I walked from the theater convinced we were all going to perish in the fire this time, right after dinner, clutching a generation's worth of draft cards and bras.

JOF (grumbling): They're going to be delayed. (Returning to the conversation): Oh, you got sucked into the story! I don't buy it; I think that Bergman was making a huge joke. Look: the movie ends with the actors in a representation of the Medieval Dance of Death. Right! Have you seen the old pictures the image refers to? Here's my phone: Check 'em out. Those thick outlines: They're cartoons!! Too bad the original mural doesn't exist anymore.

GR: There was an original mural?

JOF: Google explains that some nameless genius drew the first Dance of Death on the back wall of a Parisian cemetery in 1425, when Europe was beginning to recover from the Plague of 1348. Through wind and rain and graffiti, the mural lasted until 1669, when the wall was torn down to widen a nearby road—progress once more trumping art. Nevertheless, there are enough legacy dance-of-death representations to give a sense of what the original was like. In fact, if you want to see the tradition in action, dive into Walt Disney's first Silly Symphony, his 1929 short *The Skeleton Dance,* drawn almost entirely by the prodigious Disney Imagineer Ub Iwerks, who put together the skeletons' choreography. Talk about merriment!!

GR: The Dance of Death in *The Seventh Seal* isn't merry at all!

JOF: No. The joke is quite understated. Bergman's version of the dance—the culmination of all the scenes in which Death collects his dancers one by one—is from another tradition: the one inaugurated by the early sixteenth-century woodcut series of Hans Holbein the Younger, where one Deathmaster alone keeps popping into the busy lives of paupers and princes and popes, just a moment before they realize he's there. He retains a sense of humor, but his jokes are mostly Addams Family dry. They're directed at us, the onlookers.

MIA (to GR): Isn't Jof great! He's going into investment banking with a minor in cryptocurrency oversight, but he still has time to brush up on his art history, too. Now, I'm in poli sci, with ambitions to work in State, but I took ballet lessons during all of middle school and high school at the Jacqueline Kennedy Onassis School of American Ballet Theatre, where they pride themselves on teaching dance history. And so I can tell you that what Death dances when he's cavorting is the French line dance, the farandole. Traditionally, the farandole is a dance that's performed outdoors in a village. One man starts doing it, then he's joined by villagers of all ages, and the next thing anyone knows, the entire village has linked hands and is snaking through the streets, singing and stamping and enjoying life-enhancing exercise in wooden clogs.

JOF: During the French Revolution, when the exercise included the upper-body work of pitching the aristos into tumbrels, it was called the carmagnole; Charles Dickens has a fantastical description of it in *A Tale of Two Cities*.

MIA: In the ballet *The Sleeping Beauty*, a farandole is danced, outdoors, by members of the Prince's hunting party; unlike Aurora and her court, the Prince and his world have not been suspended from passing time, i.e., from Death. They are creatures of it.

JOF (going for a topper): And that recent dance movie *Dantza* shows a farandole in a contemporary Basque version.

MIA (crossing swords with JOF): Anyway, I think that the dance the Death figure leads at the end of *The Seventh Seal* is a variation on the farandole. (She adds slyly, buffing her nails): And like any dance in any movie, it was choreographed.

JOF (in support of MIA, exclaims): You, Girl Reporter, probably thought that the director made it up on the spot. But no!

MIA (continues): By 1957, when *The Seventh Seal* was released, Bergman was on his third wife. We ballet dancers keep track of bed partners; it can affect casting. So it wasn't until I checked Google to prepare for today's screening that I learned that Bergman's first wife, Else Fisher, had been—gadzooks!—a dancer, and that she is credited as the movie's choreographer.

Suddenly, I remembered that, in 1951, Ingmar Bergman, that gloom-and-doom helmsman, had indulged himself in confecting a ballet picture, *Summer Interlude,* about an aging ballerina who has an affair with a much-younger man. Was the movie a valediction to their marriage? And was there something more—maybe something competitive?—to Jean-Luc Godard's pronouncement that *Summer Interlude* was, in Godard's opinion, the best movie that Bergman ever made?

GR (recognizing an opening, bounds in): I'm in awe. You, Jof and Mia, could answer Mia's question definitively, yes? You have access to the 'net and search engines that translate from the Swedish and the French. You are in a position to have read documents my generation didn't know existed, to learn everything relevant to the movie and the moviemaker that can be learned! Any time, night or day, you can summon up the interview online where Bergman explains that the Knight playing chess with Death is based on a church mural by the fifteenth-century artist, embroiderer, and organist known as Albert the Painter (Albertus Pictor). You know from infancy that the "seal" in the title *The Seventh Seal* refers to the Book of Revelation. Hell, when I first heard of the movie I figured that *The Seventh Seal* must be an adventure story about a trip to the Arctic Circle. I kid you not.

JOF: Titles schmytles! We've got much more important things to think about. Bergman is a little klunky for us. Of course, we still all love Jean-Luc, his unfortunate Maoism notwithstanding. But if you really want to go "breathless," take a few gulps of the smoke from Siberia on fire or the burning forests of California.

MIA (without missing a beat): It's the subject of art, not the art of art, that matters today. And in the twenty-first century, who needs a choreographer? Learn to code and then choreograph yourself, on your phone!

JOF: We can replicate all the dancers anyone would want with CGI. Look, Bergman's stolen kisses of a summer night don't need to be projected, on real film, with an actual light source to illuminate them: they're enshrined for eternity in the pixilations of the digital universe, where everything is infinitely reproducible, and all references coexist in all languages, and you can pick up a latte 24/7—

MIA (interrupts, merrily): With the new app that supplies aroma and taste!!

JOF (clears his throat and continues): In a virtual universe, there are no limits to possibility.

MIA: Girl Reporter, have you seen the gloss on *Giselle* by the South African choreographer Dada Masilo? It goes one step beyond every other gloss on *Giselle*—Akram Khan's located in the gray world of the working class, or Mats Ek's located in a madhouse, or even Sylvie Guillem's feminist take with its twenty-six unique wedding dresses for the Wilis. Masilo's Giselle does not forget her rage at Albrecht's betrayal: she offs him with her own hand before joining the other shades, among whom is the Wili of Hilarion, Giselle's rejectee, finally getting some love! Masilo's Wilis not only wear pigeon-blood-colored tutus, they comprise individuals who identify as cis-men, as cis-women, and as every other gender classification. And the dizzying complications of dance languages—ballet for Bathilde, capoeira for the fight between Hilarion and Albrecht, the intricate rhythms of high-energy Botswana stamping dances for the Wilis—create a world of borderless crossover that is, at last, appropriate to the twenty-first century.

JOF (taking a hard breath): Yes. Audiences for this version go dead silent at the end, putting applause on hold. Indeed, there are no limits to what's possible to revise in the art of the past.

MIA (who seems not to have heard Jof, continues as if he hadn't spoken): We live in a time of radical recension, with the most radical of all being the transformation of the Earth and its inhabitants, human and animal, wrecked by climate change. Thanks a lot to you and your generation, Girl Reporter, for mucking up the entire planet! You always disparaged art that was "too literal." Well, the Big Show of Life is all literal now! Who wants even to bring children into this sorry–not sorry world you've handed down?

JOF (breathing convulsively): Me! I wanted kids!!

There is a pause for a few moments when no one speaks.

MIA (her tone softer as she tries to cool down the sitch): Look, Jof! A line of virtual souls, each arm-in-arm with an avatar, dancing along the hill.

JOF (after another moment, peering into the distance): There, at the end of the line, is the Ice Maiden, practicing her Gagaku and getting ready for her close-up! I may not be an expert in touch dancing, but I know about Ice Maidens. (Jof picks up his copy of Hans Christian Andersen's complete stories and begins to riffle through the pages.)

MIA (exasperated then rueful, unsure if she has won or lost): Oh, Jof! You and your visions.

7 lessons

As of 2022, according to the New York City Board of Education website, this is what public school students will aim to cover in the fifth grade:

- Build their vocabulary by reading more demanding books and learning new words

- Understand and use figurative language

- Explain and summarize texts while also sharing their own interpretations using evidence

- Study the use of decimals to the hundredth place

- Incorporate advanced fractions, geometry, measurements, and exponents

- Study world geography, Western cultures, early Western societies

- Learn more about earth science, including ecosystems
- Review positive health and nutrition practices

As of 1964, Miss Marion Ross White, still in her twenties and a permanent substitute fifth-grade teacher at P.S. 31, on New York's Lower East Side, was responsible to teach such "regular" fifth-grade subjects as social studies, reading, English, spelling, mathematics, geography, and science. Furthermore—as Lillian Ross put it in "Dancers in May," her masterly and meticulous fifty-six-column account of three months shadowing Miss White and her students on their educational adventures for the *New Yorker,* published that summer on July 10—for a salary of sixty-six hundred dollars for the school year, "in addition to teaching her class (which has, like all other classes at the school, a mixture of Negro and white children, with a large percentage of Puerto Ricans) . . . Miss White teaches a subject known as band." That is, she teaches the students to play one or more of these instruments: "clarinet, tuba, trumpet, trombone, saxophone, flute, bass drum, and snare drums—and then she teaches them to play in the band, of which she is the conductor. On her own time, and using her own piano, she gives free piano lessons to half a dozen children from the school. In the evening, often working past midnight, she writes her own arrangements for the band to play."

There is one more responsibility for Miss White. She and a couple of other teachers have three months to prepare a cohort of sixty fifth- and sixth-graders from P.S. 31 to learn seven European folk dances, plus an American square dance, in order for them to join some 2,740 other public-school-age mates, then known strictly as girls and boys, from forty-nine other schools to participate for one lunchtime hour, on a late spring day, in the fifty-seventh annual "Park Fête" to be held in Central Park's Sheep Meadow and in parks in each of the four other boroughs. Miss White co-teaches the dances in rehearsal on the school roof several times a week, takes some of the children to Lower East Side fabric stores for the special dance costumes and accompanying ribbons and such, and works with the volunteer mothers who make the costumes.

Finally, the day of the Park Fête arrives. The teachers and students take the subway to Columbus Circle, find their place for their school's maypole, set it up, eat their lunches from home, rest for some moments, then stand up and, at the signal, dance the dances they'd learned, in the costumes their mothers and Miss White had made, as their families and school officials watch.

Lillian Ross was a superb reporter, and school-aged children were among her most delightful subjects. She was also fascinated with film. In addition to her *New Yorker* assignment on the preparations of Miss White's class for the May Day fête, Ross worked with some young filmmakers—the Maysles brothers among them—to document the months of rehearsal and teaching and costume design. The film was edited for public television, telecast, and given a trouncing in the *New York Times* as the most boring thing ever to meet a camera lens. I went to screen it in the library at the Paley Center for Media in Midtown Manhattan, and I have to say that if I hadn't already loved "Dancers in May" on the page, I'd have been tempted to nod off here and there before the monitor; I certainly wished for some *Mad Men–*

style commercials at a few points. But what that film does is to fact-check Ross, and any questions I had while reading her about whether this or that passage was entirely reported rather than invented were answered without question. Although Ross couldn't have known that the annual May celebration by New York's public-school children would begin to wind down just as she was chronicling it; or that it would be, even so, still visible on television in the early 1970s as the backdrop to the credits for a season of *The Odd Couple,* with Oscar and Felix joining the kids to shake a leg in the park; or that, in 1999, when there were no more maypole dancers dancing, the distinguished dance-history scholar Linda J. Tomko would publish *Dancing Class,* a revelatory cultural study of the Park Fête's history—going back to its inauguration, in 1908, as an all-girls' event connected to settlement houses and progressive feminist energies and strongly influencing social service policy, women dancing on the stage, ideas concerning the promotion of healthy activities for adults and children both, the development of physical education and child-study programs, and the encouragement that children learn folk dancing for health. When, decades later, boys were finally brought into the Park Fêtes, the idea of partnered folk dancing took hold.

And then, between the 1960s and the early 1990s, American culture took a turn away from a point of view that would promote the institutionalized discipline of learning musical rhythms and coordinated steps while girls and boys simply held hands. It is unexpected and remarkable to learn that the annual May Fête of McPherson County, Kansas—celebrating the graduation of McPherson eighth graders since 1914, and complete with folk dances and Maypole—was still going strong before the Covid pandemic.

How does one evaluate a "great teacher"? If you're speaking of teachers of professional dancers, you need only look at what the person's students have accomplished. Alexander Pushkin, of the Vaganova Choreographic Institute, numbered among his students Rudolf Nureyev, Mikhail Baryshnikov, Yuri Soloviev—and other male virtuosi who went on to ballet careers that changed the art. Agrippina Vaganova herself can be similarly assessed. (Irina Kolpakova, one of the leading Auroras of her generation at the Kirov and, today, an important coach of ballerinas at American Ballet Theatre, was Vaganova's last prominent pupil in a line of illustrious ballerinas.) At the School of American Ballet, Suki Schorer—whom Balanchine brought to teaching while she was still quite young and actively performing at NYCB—has taught just about every SAB-trained ballerina of note in the past fifty years. Felia Doubrovska, Anatole Oboukov, Muriel Stuart, Stanley Williams: each of these early SAB faculty is cherished for different reasons. John Clifford—a principal dancer for Balanchine, a choreographer, a stager for the George Balanchine Trust—compared for me the teaching style of the SAB icon Antonina Tumkovsky with that of Balanchine: "Antonina Tumkovsky was a legendary teacher at Balanchine's School of American Ballet for over fifty-four years," Clifford wrote. "What made her unique was her uncompromising attention to detail combined with her fiendishly demanding exercises. Like Balanchine's classes, hers emphasized repetition to the point of exhaustion. This built an amazing stamina in all her pupils. Unlike Balanchine, she did not use metaphors to get what she wanted from students because her command of the English language was more limited; however, the combinations she put together had the same desired effect. Like Balanchine, she did not choreograph or invent new steps [in class]. They shared the ability to take the standard ballet vocabulary and put the steps together in fresh and 'dance-able' ways."

SAB is a conservatory situation, where the students already want to learn to dance. More challenging in some ways are the schools and colleges where the students have to be persuaded that dancing is worthwhile. Bettijane Sills, a former soloist with NYCB in the 1960s and a faculty member in ballet at the State University of New York at Purchase for forty-two years, wrote me a grim letter recently concerning the changes she had observed in the college—which had been founded with an emphasis on the arts. "The long-established customs of ballet training that have been handed down through generations are now being questioned and rejected," she wrote. "Furthermore, there is so much negativity floating around about Balanchine on the Internet and among students that those of us who are proponents of his style and technique and are teaching in college dance programs are in danger of becoming irrelevant."

But sometimes the dancing takes off.

When Pierre Dulaine and Yvonne Marceau—the five-time gold-medal ballroom champions at Blackpool in England and the co-founders of the short-lived and still-lamented American Ballroom Theatre—ended their dancing stint on Broadway and in London's West End, in Tommy Tune's *Grand Hotel,* Dulaine was invited by the New York City Department of Education to reintroduce partnered dancing to public schools in 1994, and his "Dancing Classrooms" program is still going strong throughout the city. Dulaine's brilliant flourish on the concept, based on an understanding of what ten- and eleven-year-olds like, was to add a citywide competition among schools, with the dressed-up finals, attended by cheerleading students and families, to anchor the semester at a fancy venue downtown. The program took off. The documentary film *Mad Hot Ballroom* (2005), which followed Dancing Classrooms into school for a season, collected warm reviews and awards at several film festivals, and Hollywood weighed in with *Take the Lead,* a feature film based on Dulaine's program, set in a New York City high school and with Dulaine's figure played by Antonio Banderas. Dulaine—born in 1944, a native of Jaffa in British Mandate Palestine who grew up in Amman, Jordan—was eventually nominated for a Nobel Prize for introducing Dancing Classrooms to schools in Jaffa (where mutually suspicious Jewish and non-Jewish students were brought, very reluctantly, to dance together) and in Northern Ireland, where he used the "Basic Six" ballroom dances to bring together, with only slightly less reluctance, students from Catholic and Protestant homes. The documentary film *Dancing in Jaffa* (2013) followed Dulaine in his efforts—a heavy lift indeed—to introduce ballroom dancing to middle-school students in the Middle East.

From here, I could take you into other dance programs in New York City, many also for fifth- and sixth-graders (one of the optimum eras of life to acquire new languages). I visited a school in Chinatown in Manhattan several times to watch the extraordinary way that the National Dance Institute, founded by New York City Ballet star Jacques d'Amboise, worked with children on dancing as a solo and an ensemble effort. There is a regulated energy in these classes that, in my experience, is unique to NDI's program and that must reflect the energy of its founder—who actually visited class at the school himself the last time I was there and brought the students to a fever pitch of enthusiasm. Over at the East Side's historic modern dance venue, the Ninety-Second Street YM-YWHA, the veteran public-schools educator, impassioned dance advocate, and well-known patron of dance Jody Gottfried Arnhold has founded the multifaceted Dance Education Laboratory.

There is the program in classical dance training in the public schools, conceived and implemented in the late 1970s by choreographer and Ballet Tech founder Eliot Feld, with dance administrator and idea marvel Cora Cahan. The program became known as the NYC Public School for Dance, and it recently hired its second artistic director in its history. In 2014, I interviewed one of its alumni, Demond Mullins. I had happened on his story in an article by Jake Abrahamson in the November 2013 issue of *Sierra* magazine, which noted that when Mullins was a soldier in Iraq, to keep his body supple he had called upon physical exercises he'd learned as a teenager when he was enrolled at the Feld-Cahan program, where he studied with American Ballet Theatre stars Christine Sarry and the choreographer Daniel Levans and, on occasion, with Richard Thomas. The *Sierra* profile also noted that, as a member of the National Guard, Mullins had "spent days guarding Penn Station with an automatic rifle," and then, on the side in his spare time, he taught dance to second-graders. (After 9/11, he was sent overseas—to Kuwait and then, for a full year, Iraq, where twice, at the request of members of his unit, he taught his fellow soldiers a dance class. In my interview with him, he described the lesson as "Martha Graham–kind of contracting and expanding of the torso, making different shapes, stretching.") Mullins had had a discouraging youth, but he did have the chance to perform with Ballet Tech. And by the time I spoke with him, he had gotten his life together, earned a B.A. in Africana studies and political science and a Ph.D. in sociology at City University, and was teaching sociology. Of what he learned in the ballet program, he told me: "Dance was the only thing I had to look forward to. Dance is 99 percent busting your ass for 1 percent in the limelight. Most of the time I was dancing I was clinically depressed, but dance almost put me in another state of being. It was incredible to be able to step outside of myself."

That out-of-body feeling Mullins describes as what dance can effect was also referred to in interviews I conducted with the Jordanian dancer Bijan Qutub—a business school student of some three hundred pounds who decided to take up ballet, lost half his body weight in doing so, and realized that he wanted to become a professional dancer. Before the pandemic, I saw him perform with the Joffrey School in New York—both jazz dancing and a duet, in which he proved an excellent partner. His physical transformation into a true professional-level dancer—entirely self-generated—would not have been possible if dancing had not given him the feeling of flow. Photographs of Bijan's journey in dance are available on the internet.

From a very different corner of the dance world, Sally Hess—the choreographer and erstwhile performer with Dan Wagoner and faculty member in dance at Swarthmore College and Princeton University—has also spoken about the extraordinary feeling that dancing well conveys, even with pain in one's joints and other physical complaints. The sense of well-being may be so strong that performance becomes a way station in a process rather than a destination. In her late seventies, Sally (a friend of mine since 1970) was given some ballroom dance classes at the West Seventy-Second Street Fred Astaire studio. She tried it, found it interesting, kept at it, and now plans her entire schedule around ballroom dancing. Her principal teachers these days are the studio's co-owners, tall and commanding Darius and Jolanta Mosteika, themselves winners of international competitions. (Their competition programs are available online.) I have been to many of Sally's classes with them—observing how she learns different things from each. (Jolanta serves as a coach for Sally and Darius, taking on the role of a leader or a follower, as necessary, to demonstrate her notes.) At this advanced level of ballroom dancing, the mission is beyond learning the steps: it is to try to find a common breath and a mutual heartbeat for the dancing couple as, at tempo, they spiral through cascading musical counts in the Viennese waltz; the most delicate shiftings of weight are critical.

I have also seen Sally and Darius perform in showcases and, via film, in competitions, where they invariably are awarded gold medals. Some of the movements they perform are unique to them. What makes them truly special though, is that their dancing looks completely spontaneous, in the moment. That look, at least in American dance, is what, to me, reveals contact with teachers of rarefied excellence, such as the Balanchine light-bringer Suki Schorer, or, in modern dance, the late Bella Lewitzky (a mainstay of Lester Horton's rigorous technique, important for Alvin Ailey's dancers), or the tap stylist Charles "Honi" Coles, whose impeccable ear and analytic gifts—and personal kindness—made it possible for even a seasoned tap choreographer of merit such as Brenda Bufalino to open herself to learning like a child. The kind of study that my friend Sally is doing with the Mosteikas is a form of cultural privilege: as Demond Mullins remembered, even in the midst of personal turmoil, such study makes one glad to be alive.

Although the rule of thumb is that one cannot learn to dance from a book (or an electronic equivalent), every rule has its exception. Here is a gift to readers who might like to learn a dance in the privacy of your own home or office.

In 1979, Merce Cunningham choreographed a solo on his own body, made up of fifty "positions" (Cunningham's word, rather than "poses"), called *Fifty Looks.* To connect the "looks," he devised rules. Late in 2020, Patricia Lent, the director of licensing for the Merce Cunningham Trust (who, in addition to being a treasured alumna of the Cunningham company, is also a veteran, full-time teacher of academic subjects in the New York City public schools), studied Cunningham's notes for *Fifty Looks,* along with a film of Cunningham performing the work and archival notes and materials he generated in developing the dance. Then, in order to teach *Fifty Looks* for free to the public (regardless of how much or how little experience one may have had with any kind of dance), she put on Vimeo the notes, film, photos of herself in each position, and other materials relevant to how *Fifty Looks* was made using chance operations. In three sessions, still posted on the website for the Cunningham Trust, you, reader, can learn this Cunningham solo as an entity—as something separate from the way it looked on Cunningham's body in performance of it. (A collateral benefit is that, in effect, you learn to embody one answer to the famous question at the end of "Among School Children," W. B. Yeats's poem about the balance between nature and culture: "How can we know the dancer from the dance?" Do it yourself!)

Months later, in response to Lent's generous posting, the dance critic Marina Harss—not a professional dancer but someone who takes ballet lessons as an adult—wrote an article for the *New York Times,* "Twist, Bend, Reach, Step" (April 21, 2020), about her own efforts to bring the positions into her own body; the fifty illustrations are demonstrated by another person, the photographer Camila Falquez, in a fire-engine red jumpsuit.

Harss writes:

> The solo is possibly his plainest, almost an ABC of his meticulous approach to subdividing the body in motion—twist, bend, reach, step. You don't need a large area, just a few square feet. For the most part, it moves forward in space.
>
>   . . .

In many ways, learning and executing these simple steps is like a meditation, performed in silence.

Twyla Tharp has devised a similar process to teach dancers and non-dancers her early work called *The One Hundreds,* which can be performed by one hundred amateurs, each learning one unique eleven-second phrase taught by a Tharp dancer, plus various other combinations of performers—for instance, by ten experienced dancers, each performing ten eleven-second phrases; or by a first-rate soloist (or an ensemble of such soloists), performing the full one hundred eleven-second phrases. In the *New Yorker* issue of July 6 and 13, 2015, the non-dancing literary critic and art historian Claudia Roth Pierpont (who looks so much like a dancer that Balanchine once asked if she was one) published her article "The Horde," reporting on one anonymous amateur who, for a special Tharp event, effectively incorporated his cane into a high-arm gesture: "The arm thrust was part of the sequence, and the cane added a kind of exclamation point," Pierpont writes, "but what Tharp congratulated him on, with the hint of a grin herself, was finishing on the count of eleven, just in time." Tharp's stopwatch standard of execution links her to Cunningham. For these choreographers, and for many others, the meaning of a dance moment is a matter of time in the literal sense of minutage, over and above pictorial imagery. That said, although such meaning is embodied in designed movement, even the choreographer may not be able to discuss its identity and implications in a concise way.

As the American choreographer Pam Tanowitz told Lyndsey

Winship, a reporter for the *Guardian,* on April 11, 2019, regarding her enthusiastically heralded evening-length, storyless dance to *Four Quartets,* T. S. Eliot's poetic rumination on the nature of time and eternity, read aloud—a work that Tanowitz pored over for decades on the page before she took two years to choreograph it as if it were music—"I still don't understand the poem," explaining that it will mean different things at different moments in one's life. Her wonderment did not stop her from making a *Four Quartets* dance, though. In an interview with Gia Kourlas of the *New York Times,* printed on July 4, 2018, Tanowitz explained that, whether one understands it or not, Eliot's poem is "inevitable. As it goes on, you don't question anything." She adds, "So I'm letting the dance show me what to do. If I can do that and make it seem inevitable, then maybe I can even have 2 percent of what he did in this poem."

epilogue

I was thinking that maybe someone leafing through this book would be what I'd call young, that is, no older than the late twenties—or even younger than that: college age or a high school senior. Would it be relevant at all to the issues of that person's moment? We live in radically transforming times, not yet as encompassing as the sweeps of humanity in 1789 or 1917 or 1939 or 1949, but insidious, and possibly irreversible, with the very ground we tread and the very air we breathe and the very water that we guzzle to replenish our cells deteriorating and poisoned in conditions our species has devised. What will happen to my child, her husband, and their child? In this little book, I offer up to them and to their generations a personal story I've cobbled together of dance, a sometime human activity and a niche art. What kind of gift is that? Wouldn't a story of why food and waste management matter be more useful? Of marine biology? Of fundraising and crowd sourcing for the preservation of civic elections?

In his 1956 masterpiece *A Treatise on Poetry,* the great Lithuanian-born poet Czesław Miłosz calls down the heavens on the generation of Polish poets he grew up reading, a group annihilated by the Nazis—who liked to plaster each mouth shut before putting a bullet in each brain—for having selfishly focused on beauty and aesthetics in their work rather than assisting Miłosz's generation by using their poets' radar to point to the signs of the infernal world to come. And yet, here, now, what Miłosz saw as a choice may no longer be one. Earlier, I touched on the publications regarding beauty by our contemporary Umberto Eco (b. 1932). In 2020, the English translation was published of his handy-dandy self-helper *How to Spot a Fascist,* one of whose three essays contains a checklist of characteristics that the author learned about close at hand from growing up in the Italy of Benito Mussolini. Transparent Beauty and Dark Knowledge: With luck and perseverance, one person can provide them both.

In 1959, some twenty years before Eco brought out his first novel, the hit known in English as *The Name of the Rose,* he published in his native Italian a small yet pithy book about the philosophical and ecclesiastical debates of the Middle Ages and early Renaissance concerning the physical properties and spiritual meaning of beauty. Its English translation by Hugh Bredin, delayed until 1986, entitled it *Art and Beauty in the Middle Ages,* and although it's not quite a beach read, I highly commend it, especially if you're willing to, so to speak, put your mind to the grindstone in an effort to understand why the figure of the Sleeping Beauty trails centuries of abstract thought behind her with every pas de bourrée. Umberto Eco is a literary phenomenon—

famous, learned, imaginative, amusing, and popular, too. Nevertheless, one wouldn't expect that his early immersion in medieval studies would so enchant his commanding officer during his military service as to convert the lieutenant into a philosophical protector. The following anecdote is from the preface to *Art and Beauty in the Middle Ages:*

> As soon as I agreed to write this text, I had to spend eighteen months in the Italian Army. I am ever grateful to the lieutenant that gave me the daily opportunity to leave the barracks for the shelter of the comfortable library. Moreover, he provided me with a small office where I put all my books and files, as well as my typewriter . . . , and there I could work peacefully. I was a private and the lieutenant acted as my janitor, telling the intruders: "don't disturb, professor at work." I was so absorbed by medieval aesthetics that one day I lost my gun and I do not remember how and why I escaped the firing squad. But I was, as I still am, a bellicose pacifist.

I find this an unusual story for the military and for literature, although I simply may not know enough about either and should be glad if someone who does would prove me wrong. However, I do know that dancing of every tradition is filled with stories of non-dancing helpers who made the dance possible. Many of them are parents of aspiring dancers. A colleague of mine used to say that she intended to write a book about dance mothers—the kind who, like the mother of Fred and Adele Astaire, gave up nearly everything, including her marriage, to take her talented children from their native Nebraska to New York to study dancing and to perform it professionally. There could be a second large volume on dance teachers and gurus around the world, beginning with outstanding examples in India. Producers and impresarios, donors and patrons, even some critics, would populate a third volume, such as Anna Kisselgoff, whose reportorial writings on behalf of the Paul Taylor Dance Company, which was in dire financial straits at one point, kept the financial woes of the organization and the choreographer before readers until the company was rescued. (Lincoln Kirstein's assistance to dancing and dancers goes so far beyond his bringing Balanchine to the United States and, with him, co-founding several companies and the School of American Ballet as to earn Kirstein a chapter unto himself. Sometimes publicly but often silently, in myriad ways, he provided cash and crucial connections to dancers, choreographers, writers, artists, designers, publishers, editors, libraries. His life in the arts in America is summed up by the word "irreplaceable.")

The downside of dancing as an art or even as a pastime is that so many individuals are needed to put it on and maintain the venues, as well as the other personnel involved, as to make dance a budget-buster, always on the edge of bankruptcy. When you read about the luxe ideals, aesthetic and intellectual, that Serge Diaghilev kept before him, and the Herculean energies he had to expend to acquire the resources to embody them on stage, you might conclude—instead of comparing his Ballets Russes to the Paris Opéra Ballet, the Bolshoi, and the Mariinsky, which enjoy hundreds of years of existence as well as government patronage and their own theaters, or to the eighty-three-year-old American Ballet Theatre or the seventy-five-year-old New York City Ballet—that it was utterly amazing for Diaghilev to keep his uniquely creative experiment going for even the score of years that it lasted. He made astounding, historic opportunities possible for the most brilliant of choreographers, composers, artists, and dancers, but despite loyal assistants and a roster of outstanding artists and audiences who were still game for the next unpredictable ballet, he had no sustaining patron to relieve him of the parts of keeping the company alive that weren't fun, that were perhaps at times humiliating as well as anxiety-producing. When he sickened and died, in 1929, having lost his enthusiasm for ballet and retreated into his bibliophile's library, the company immediately vanished. He and he alone had been its heartbeat. Could you do it? I couldn't.

Another story about the kind of help that dancers require and, with luck, can enjoy, is one I heard several years ago during a live session at a symposium on dance at Hunter College, where it was related by Joan Myers Brown, the distinguished teacher and much-honored founder of the modern-dance-based Philadelphia Dance Company, known as Philadanco. I've never met her, but I've felt as if we'd encountered one another in some previous life ever since I read about her in Brenda Dixon Gottschild's *Joan Myers Brown and the Audacious Hope of the Black Ballerina: A Biohistory of American Performance* (2011). We are about the same age, both only children reared in Philadelphia, both deeply smitten by classical ballet, and both of us greatly disappointed by aspects of our ballet dreams. But her disappointment was worse, for it was not only painful but unfair. Joan Myers Brown has a slender frame and smooth muscles and a body beautifully proportioned for classical dancing. She was fortunate to have studied with esteemed African American teachers of ballet such as Essie

Marie Dorsey and Marion Durham Cuyjet, yet she wasn't able to pursue a classical career in the 1950s and 1960s: not only was she African American but her skin tone was too dark for her to pass for white, even if she had, as paler Cuyjet temporarily seemed to do for a while at the Littlefield School. At Hunter, Joan Myers Brown explained that the choreographer Antony Tudor used to travel weekly to Philly from New York to teach at the Center City studio of Thomas Cannon. She would study with Tudor there—and during classes in partnering, Tudor would choose her as his partner. As she related her feeling at his having done so, it was a kind of blessing that endowed her with an underground glow throughout her career.

But this miracle was owing, in addition to her personal dancerly gifts, to a remarkable network of helpers. Tudor, who could be so cruel to students that he reduced them to tears in class, was fair, even noble here. Thomas Cannon—ballet master for Catherine Littlefield, of Philadelphia's all-white Littlefield Ballet—was, himself, willing to teach students of color. As both Gottschild's book and Theresa Ruth Howard's indispensable website MoB Ballet.org ("Curating the Memoirs of Blacks in Ballet") explain, after the light-skinned Marion Cuyjet was dismissed from the Littlefield School, in the 1940s, Cuyjet's original teacher, Essie Marie Dorsey, paid Cannon to teach Cuyjet privately. During the 1950s, Tudor made his weekly teaching trips to Cannon's studio in Center City (the Littlefield Ballet had been disbanded after the bombing of Pearl Harbor, in 1941, when the company's male dancers were called up by the draft). It was in the later 1950s when Joan Myers Brown, who studied with Cuyjet and Cuyjet's mentor, Dorsey, took the classes by Tudor at Cannon's. All those people having to organize, fund, and participate in a segregated system in order to bring a couple of talented students to study what Nature and their own abilities and desires had ideally fitted them to do. It's exhausting just to contemplate, as well as being horrifically immoral from a spiritual standpoint and, from a practical one, inefficient.

A couple of years ago, I had the honor to fill in as a teacher of dance history in a performing arts conservatory. During that semester, the class—a considerable percentage of whom were students of color—spent one period explaining to me how onerous it was for them to be there and how boring it was for them to take all these Balanchine-type ballet classes. Better to be in Europe, several concluded. They unpacked their reasons, and given their experiences and the surrounding culture, some of those reasons almost made sense to me, at least for them. On the other hand, it was in that hour when I was brought to understand that I faced them from across a Grand Canyon–sized generational divide of cultural expectations.

The ballet that Joan Myers Brown would have loved to have danced in, she said to her largely gray-haired audience at Hunter, was Michel Fokine's *Les Sylphides,* set to Chopin in a forest glade, where the corps and female principals nested around the ballet's lone male soloist (originally Nijinsky) are on pointe and in long, Romantic tutus. This dream indicates a dreamer far more sophisticated about ballet than I was at that time. As a teenage after-school ballet student, I had enjoyed my ten weekly classes with my own Center City teacher, Pete Conlow, for his ability to impart basic principles of classical ballet in a pure, unmannered way and for his help in bringing forward the gifts of outstanding dancers (Jill Malamud, Warren Conover, the adolescent Nina Fedorova). However, listening to those stories at Hunter, I realized that all the while I was practicing pirouettes and entrechats at Pete's studio under the illusion I might become a dancer, Joan Myers Brown—who really *was* a dancer, with one of the world's finest choreographers as her weekly partner—was subject to unimaginable unfairness. And yet she persisted in dance, eventually founding Philadanco and becoming someone who helped many others to performing careers as she would have wanted to have been helped. Even though her company will probably never perform *Les Sylphides,* its founder will always be a living example of the adage that when one door closes another opens, a perspective on living that doesn't always obtain but that can keep someone going, at least for a while, when the literal doors and windows are no longer available.

Regardless of what form it takes, dancing is a calling. It animates individuals, those who practice it and those who obsessively follow it from afar. Nevertheless, when you see a dancer in any tradition realize all that is in that person to realize, you are inevitably in the presences, too, of the unseen persons who contributed assistance. Petipa dramatized them as the Fairies who bring endowments to the infant Aurora in the Prologue of *The Sleeping Beauty.* In doing so, he also presented an important truth about the essentially social nature of dance (even, one might add, a highly individual dance practice like Sufi spinning, where each dancer revolves on a personal axis while surrounded by a galaxy of collegial human planets who are similarly revolving).

If you read *Revelations* (1995), the autobiography of Alvin Ailey (written with A. Peter Bailey), you'll find an account of a comparable yet limited situation to that of the young Joan Myers Brown, with the racial terms reversed: where she, an African American classicist, dreamed of performing in *Les Sylphides,* a ballet that traditionally showcases white dancers in gossamer white dresses to the music of the ultimate white Romantic, Ailey recounts the dream of a white classicist in his company to dance the solo he subtitled as his honor for Black women everywhere. She was a classicist he valued and whom he cast in leading parts, including the lead in his *Memoria,* a work he made to celebrate the life of his beloved friend the choreographer Joyce Trisler, who died lamentably young. Yet these two dreams are not equivalent—that of an African American dancer longing to perform in a beautiful fantasy and that of a white dancer longing to perform in a work made for the birthday of the choreographer's mother, who was quite alive when it was finished and in the audience to see its first performance.

Ailey always opened his company to a few excellent dancers—men and women—who were not African American. One of them was the white dancer I just mentioned, an outstanding company principal with a film star's physical appeal. She asked Ailey if she could learn and perform his sixteen-minute, program-stopping solo *Cry* (1971), dedicated to "all Black women everywhere—especially our mothers." *Cry* was made on the statuesque star (and native Philadelphian) Judith Jamison, and I first saw her dance it, soon after its premiere, in the Walnut Street Theater in Philadelphia. In her own memoir, *Dancing Spirit* (1993), Jamison explains that the solo was intended as a birthday present for Ailey's mother, who was coming to New York from Texas to see her child's celebrated dance company and who would be experiencing her birthday during her trip. "In those days, none of us could shop at Tiffany or Bloomingdale's," Jamison writes, "so Alvin decided that the nicest present he could give his mother was a ballet."

As Ailey tells the story, the white dancer did not understand that what she was asking for went beyond nontraditional or colorblind casting: she did not take into account that the identity of the soloist—as a woman and as an African American—was an irreducible core element of Ailey's dance, no less than any individual gesture or leap. To permit a white female soloist to perform *Cry* (or any male soloist, one presumes) was not the same as a bravura Asian tap dancer cast in, say, *42nd Street,* or Scandinavian experts in Argentine tango starring in a tango revue in Saint Petersburg, or a Vietnamese ballerina taking the role of Swanilda in a Ho Chi Minh City production of *Coppélia.* The issue is also not that only Judith Jamison, for whom *Cry* was made, should have performed it. The world has seen more than a few remarkable soloists in *Cry,* including the stunningly beautiful and virtuosic Donna Wood; in the December 2021 Ailey season at New York's City Center theater, I saw a breathtaking performance of the solo by the then-current Ailey dancer Jacqueline Green, who had been coached by both Jamison and Wood, in a new staging by the longstanding Ailey associate artistic director Masazumi Chaya. Green's identity as an African American is not what made her performance astonishing: her dancing did that. Still, her African American identity was no less part of the text of the dance than the key movements on which its choreography depends.

However, the white dancer's request here throws into relief other modern dances and ballets where there is a discrepancy between a character's physical appearance and a dancer's identity as a person. Perhaps the most highly valued dance and performance on film by José Limón, a naturalized American of Mexican descent, is his appearance in the title role of his work *The Moor's Pavane,* a compression of Shakespeare's *Othello.* When it has been performed by other companies—or by the choreographer's own since his death—the casting very rarely features an African American male dancer as the Moor. Should the historic film with Limón's Moor be suppressed? Should *The Moor's Pavane,* absent an African American Moor, be suppressed? Fokine's powerful ballet masterpiece *Petrouchka,* which features another Moor as a supporting character, a cruel one, has not been performed, to my knowledge, in this century by any of the American or European companies where it is part of the longstanding repertory. Yet all of its roles are so challenging and provocative, and its Stravinsky score and Alexandre Benois designs are so fantastical, and the poetic questions posed by the story concerning authoritarianism and free will are so relevant that the idea of *Petrouchka* being lost to future dancers and audiences is deeply troubling, especially given the fact that the greatest executant of the clown-white title role I ever saw—the Joffrey Ballet's Gary Chryst, celebrated by audiences and his peers within the profession of ballet—is himself a dancer of color.

But this discussion concerns characters of fantasy. What about ballets exclusively populated by historic personages, such as Ashton's *Enigma Variations,* with the composer Edward Elgar, his wife, and their friends? Cis-gender men and trans women whose sex at birth was identified as male are now performing professionally on pointe—not in a comic mode, like the hilarious Trocks, but earnestly, sometimes wearing classical tutus as well; at least one new pointe shoe company, geared to masculine feet, has been established to serve them. By the end of this century will the world's leading ballet academies routinely be training them in its pointe classes and casting them in the ballerina parts of Balanchine ballets? As Mrs. Elgar? I ask these questions seriously, and I have no crystal ball to produce answers, any more than I can predict the long-range changes to dance that will be wrought by Covid-19. Indeed, given the extraordinary advances in film and communications technology, will it one day be possible for a hologram of Rudolf Nureyev to perform Ailey's *Cry,* and will a distinction be made in the dance world and among its audiences, then, between the capability for that to happen and the choreographer's wishes, back at the end of the twentieth century, as to whether it *should* happen?

I close with *Hard to Be Soft—A Belfast Prayer,* a postmodern dance-theater work of less than an hour created in 2017 by Oona Doherty, the thirty-six-year-old Belfast choreographer already being celebrated in Europe for the power, structural invention, and emotional charge of her dance and movement theater. In a two-week run during January 2022, *Hard to Be Soft* was performed at the Irish Art Center in New York by Doherty, her core collaborators from Ireland, and a group of young women Doherty calls the Sugar Army (recruited locally wherever this work is performed; in New York, the army came from a group of dancers who shared a summer experience called the Young Dancemakers Company, for public high school students).

I caught up with it a couple of weeks before the fiftieth anniversary of Bloody Sunday. Although I'd been prepared by Siobhan Burke's carefully detailed advance piece of January 10, 2022, in the *New York Times,* for Doherty's theme of Northern Irish workingmen, stirred by the thirty-year Troubles to alternative bouts of fury and attempts at healing with one another, I was startled by how each of the four brief sections immediately seized attention through transformations ascribable to movement and, in the cases of Doherty's two bookending solos, to a kind of dance acting I don't remember having seen since Baryshnikov performed the Leonid Jacobson solo *Vestris,* which featured a series of distinct characters rolling from the dancer's body into the clarifying light of a sparely dressed stage. The section with the Sugar Army employed geometric arrangements of the dancing schoolgirls, each wearing a sparkly shirt in an individual paintbox color and each performing with her own distinct personality as a dancer while participating in the ensembles, convening in space according to common counts. At the last moment of the section, all but one of the girls has paraded away out of sight, and that orphan turns to peer, with increasing curiosity, upstage into a strip of lighting between a wall of slats, as if something untoward was gradually being revealed. It was like turning the page at the end of one story in *Dubliners* to land at the opening of the next one, and the stage effect was a little coup de théâtre: this working-class Belfast of Doherty's turned out to be a collective of individualities, permitting not only the choreographer-star but also a schoolgirl to take center stage in her own private discovery.

The third section, for two barefoot, shirtless men—here, Sam Finnegan and the choreographer John Scott, both of ample girth, their bellies oozing over the waistbands of their trousers—presents images of assault and tenderness, now with the men slanted isometrically against one another, and now, in rehearsal for their final grave beds, lying side by side on the floor, a total engagement of physiques and psyches. The audience can, if focused, really feel the many facets of the Troubles via this pair, their glistening skin bonding themselves now like frenemies, now like animals in mutual assault, now like intimates wrestling playfully, and then for real.

Doherty's second solo ends with a choral recitation of a prayer on the sound score by David Holmes, a prayer for healing. That was made four or five years ago; in the *Times* interview with Burke, the choreographer expresses some uncertainty as to whether dance can actually heal anything. If one doesn't countenance beauty, the glance down the time tunnel to try to see what will happen to dance with Doherty, or artists of her perspective, yields a vision that, to me, looks related to the worlds of Samuel Beckett: lots of life springing from pain; humor birthed in miseries; loveliness teetering on youth like a porcelain plate momentarily balanced on edge; a societal conscience underwriting the imagery (no art for art's sake); sound that occupies the same running time as the movement but is emotionally independent of it, as in offstage life. Most important to the dances of the future will be the dance makers' ability to ensure that the audiences who ruminatively make their way out of the theater at the end are different inside themselves from those audiences who ambled in.

In May 2016, Doherty published a statement, in the online publication *DRAFF*, called "Hard to be soft," which concludes:

> I'm motivated to create rough and pure dance. That smashes laziness into the ground with a dedication to a truthful body. To bring the sex and the punk back into the black box, the white cube, the body. Ireland.
>
> Here's to a weightless milky future kidz.

Certainly, the future will hold much more for dance than this; however, if we're lucky, it will not hold less.

The book you have read was completed just before Russia invaded Ukraine, targeting civilians and destroying or heavily damaging some fifteen hundred buildings so far, including hospitals, museums, and theaters. Owing to the conscription of able-bodied Ukrainian men between eighteen and sixty years of age, many of the civilian murders have been of children, women, the elderly, and the physically challenged. Photographs of the port city of Mariupol, pounded flat by Russian shelling, resemble a moonscape. Yet Russia's invading army has experienced four- to five-figure losses inflicted by the defending Ukrainians—whose bravery has astonished the world and galvanized much of the West to render assistance.

Among the militarized defenders are dancers, ballet dancers in most cases, women as well as men. At least one—the Ukrainian ballet star Artem Datsyshyn—has died under artillery fire. Also, professional ballet dancers in Russia, disgusted with the war, have spoken out against the Putin regime that is conducting it and have left for other countries; among them are Russian ballerinas, including the prodigious and beautiful, Vaganova-schooled Olga Smirnova, who was immediately engaged by the Dutch National Ballet. Two entire ballet companies from Ukraine, one on tour in Europe and one in the United States, are stranded abroad. As I write, efforts throughout the West are being made to try to assist them and Ukrainian dancers who arrived individually, including through the offer of jobs as performers, even though there are few such jobs to be had at this time of year; even though a job for a refugee, while providing one kind of diversity, forecloses other kinds; and even though—as the critic Alastair Macaulay has pointed out to Rebecca King Ferraro and Michael Sean Breeden, in their podcast *Conversations on Dance*—the aesthetics and training of the Ukrainian or Russian refugee dancers might prove inharmonious or unpalatable to a Western company, however much that organization might wish to assist the refugees for humanitarian reasons.

Meanwhile, as the critic Marina Harss reported in the *New York Times,* the revered Russian-born and Kyiv-reared choreographer Alexei Ratmansky (whose birth family is in Kyiv, as is the family of his wife, Tatiana, who is Ukrainian) has at least temporarily abandoned a large ballet he was working on at the Bolshoi, set to Bach's *Art of the Fugue,* and perhaps permanently abandoned an extravagant, historically informed production he was planning for the Mariinsky of the Marius Petipa ballet-spectacle *The Pharaoh's Daughter.* Online, Ratmansky also challenged the view of the even more revered native Latvian and Russian-reared dancer and actor Mikhail Baryshnikov, who registered opposition to the requirement among some U.S. performing arts organizations that, in order to continue to appear in their productions, visiting Russian artists must go on record as condemning the war Vladimir Putin's army is waging in Ukraine. Baryshnikov spoke of possible fears on the part of those artists of reprisal against their families in Russia, against which Ratmansky cited particular artists who had already signed public letters, in 2014, to endorse the Russian army's incursions into and annexation of Crimea. Both men condemn what the army has done to Ukraine, and both men have U.S. citizenship; however, it is Baryshnikov who, a defector from Russia, speaks up on behalf of First Amendment issues, while Ratmansky, who settled in New York without drama, is the debater who, as Macaulay put it approvingly in a social media post, "names names," a phrase (and an action) that, for a segment of the American public, still carries a whiff of the House Un-American Activities Committee and its notorious blacklist.

Still, we are not living in the late 1940s. The government that wielded the HUAC blacklist as a brute cudgel now makes at least some distinctions (such as the no-fly lists for commercial flight); it is the culture at large that now spreads blanket cancellations. Furthermore, even though, given the tragedy in Ukraine that is intensifying momentarily, dancing is hardly a priority in the general news, the bravery, independence, nimble intelligence, and, most of all, capacity for leadership of the country's elected president, Volodymyr Zelensky, would not be likely to surprise anyone who studied the short compendium of filmed moments from the many dances that he and his partner aced in the 2006 edition of Ukraine's version of *Dancing with the Stars* (available on the website of the *New York Post*). Dancing isolates certain aspects of an individual's way of negotiating challenges that, in other contexts, could become transformed into, and energize, nontheatrical elements of personality and societal initiative. These aspects and elements are not frozen but rather respond to changes in their environment. *How* that response affects a person's choices is an ethical and aesthetic matter to be interpreted and evaluated. Yet quite separate is the *ability to respond* instantly to different conditions while continuing in one's core mission: it is that ability—neurological and psychic—that links a person most strongly to what makes dance dance.

Whatever will have happened by the time my book is in your hands, the performance of Zelensky and his partner for the show, the professional dancer Olena Shoptenko, in a number where both were blindfolded and apparently negotiated the supper club–style, touch-dance choreography by silently counting, will be—for this ink-stain'd wretch of dance writing who is, for several reasons, against blacklists—an achievement worth terming visionary.

acknowledgments

This book exists for two reasons. The first is because a former Yale University Press editor, the nimble intellectual Steve Wasserman, son of a dancer, thought the art worthy of inclusion in the "Why X Matters" series. Decades earlier, Steve tried to wrest a book from me for a different press; this time he was victorious. Before westering back to his native Berkeley to become the publisher of Heyday Books, he invited me to be the author of the entry on dance. We all thought it would be a walk in the park to produce, and it was—a walk in a very big park, which took more than ten years. During that time, I worked at many different jobs to keep body and soul hale and shod. The writing was also not a typical process for me; it seemed to come from a strange place psychically—as if it were being given. I didn't quite trust it, which also probably drew out the experience. Yet friends, family, colleagues, and—I was surprised to find looking back—memories of particular students helped the words flow. Many persons also helped me directly, sometimes through offering ideas (or sparking mine); sometimes by continuing to ask why? or by tenaciously disagreeing; sometimes by repairing my body as it fell apart; sometimes through sharing their stories in dance; sometimes in making research materials accessible; sometimes by making it possible for me to go to the theater; and, in a few instances, by subsidizing my rent or utility bills now and then, as, once, in other circumstances, I was able to help different friends who were down on their luck. Just to get the book going took a village.

I am grateful to the critic and historian Robert Greskovic and the cultural historian Gilbert Gaytan, who made time to read a completed chapter of this book for factual accuracy. After the manuscript was submitted to the publisher, the historian Martha Ullman West read the entire manuscript "for fun"—and caught some things. My daughter, Ariel Cohen, kindly scrutinized the Epilogue.

However, only one person served as a reader while the writing was in process and could have been fundamentally restructured: Robert Gottlieb, who perused most of the chapters early on because he asked to read them. I have been edited formally by Bob (when he headed up the *New Yorker*) and enjoyed his formidable assistance on a recent Library of America anthology I edited on dance, including our collaborative proofreading sessions of the entire volume. However, his reading of my work here was done from friendship and his own curiosity about these essays on dancing, a subject that has mattered to him very much since his first view, as a high school student, of George Balanchine's *Orpheus* with its original cast. I've never written anything this long and unpredictable. Bob's soft-spoken attention encouraged me to persist as I had begun; he led me to feel that what I was writing might be of some use. Without his interest I'd have thrown in the towel long ago.

All gratitude to the hardworking staff who shepherded the manuscript through peer review, permissions, and production at Yale University Press: Director John Donatich, Editorial Director Seth Ditchik, Managing Editor Dorothea Halliday, Designer Sonia Shannon, Copy Editor Laura Jones Dooley, Indexer Meridith Murray, and, with my special appreciation, Editorial Assistants Amanda Gerstenfeld and Eva Skewes.

A révérence to the knee for the dedicated staffs of the libraries and archives I consulted. At the Jerome Robbins Dance Division of the New York Public Library for the Performing Arts: Linda Murray (Director), Arlene Yu, Tanisha Jones, Daisy Pommer, Phil Karg, Erik Stolarski, Cassie Mey, Alice Standin, Tasha Agard, Kenneth Murphy, Jessica Gavilan, Suzanne Lipkin, Jennifer Eberhardt, and Nailah Holmes. At the Brooklyn Academy of Music Archives: Louie Fleck. And the Paley Archive at the Paley Center for Media in Midtown Manhattan.

I am deeply thankful to the following individuals who gave up their time to be interviewed for this book or who gave permission for me to quote within it extended passages of their writing: Joan Acocella, John Clifford, Jonathan Cott, Senta Driver, Robert Garland, the Estate of David Gordon, Joseph Houseal, Yuriko Kikuchi and Emiko Tokunaga, Esther Kontarsky, Michael Manswell, Demond Mullins, Claudia Roth Pierpont, Michelle Potter, Bettijane Sills, Bijan Qutub.

Amy Sun and Shannon Harmer represented PARS International.

Some individuals I salute for their inspiration and kindness whose names are not in the text: Jake Abrahamson, the Abramson Family, Robert Abrams, Carolyn Adams, Morgan Albahary, Michael and Kelly Album, the late William Alpert, Cage Ames, Jack Anderson, the late Olga Andrejev, Miriam Arsham, Atsede Assayehgen, William Ausman, Meredith Babb, Richard Bailey, Ansie Baird, the late Valerie Taylor Barnes, Eleanor Barrisser, Aileen Barry, Linda Bathgate, Zachary Bloomgarden, Friedrich Boettner, Book Group, Amy Bordy, the late Ruthanna Boris, Frauke Breede, Ed Brill, Matthew Brookoff, Lynn Matluck Brooks, Joy Williams Brown, the late Winfred Parker Buckwalter III, Lenka Burke, Marcus Burke, Diana Byer, Christopher Caines, Maguette Camara, Justin Cammy, John Canemaker, Steven Caras, Suzanne Carbonneau, Mary Cargill, Meryl Cates, Rebecca Chaleff, Aaqilah Chambers, the late Marge Champion, Sophie Flack Charles, Angela Chi, Sera Chen, the late Mary Cochran, Marty Cohen and family, the late Selma Jeanne Cohen, Ze'eva Cohen, the late Karyn Collins, the Columbia Seminars, Joel Conarroe, Rachel Cooper, Uttara Coorlawala, Robert Cornfield, Robert Craft Esq., Duke Dang, Rob Daniels, the late Henry Danton, Elysia Dawn, the late Gemze de Lappe, Christie DeMarchi, Mariama Diagne, Alyse Dissette, the late Virginia Donaldson, George Dorris, Sophia Dougherty, Irene Dowd, Trudi Down (the Book Band), Kevin Doyle, Siobhan Dunham, Ruth Eshel, the late John Esten, the late Jinx Falkenburg, Diana Fanizza, Margot Fein, Brittany Rose Feit, Irving Feldman, the late Barbara

Milberg Fisher, Georgette Fleischer, Marjorie Folkman, Alisa Forman, Suzannah Friscia, Carlos Garcia, Sarah Garcia, Sarah Garvey, Beth Genné, Mary Meeker Gesek, the late Leslie Getz, Allan Gibbard, the late Alice and the late William Gifford, Katie Glasner, Lynn Glauber, Mildred Goldczer, Gail and Zvi Golod, John A. Goodman Jr., Ain Gordon, the late Beate Gordon, Elena Gordon, Ayalah Goren-Kadman, Gloria Gottschalk, Cameron Grant, Jonathan Gray, Jonnie Greene and Family, Sanford Greene, Allen Greenberg, Karen Greenspan, Nancy Groppern, the late Dennis Grunes, Ann Hutchinson Guest, Maureen Gupta, Jeffrey (Gus) Gustafson, Hila Gutfreund, Joe Guttridge, Julia Hammid, Grace Hargis, the late James Harvey, Kena Herod, Linden Hill, Trish Hoard, Ayala Hochman, Annabelle Hochschild, Stuart Hodes, Christian Holder, Nawshin Hoque, Christopher Howell, Reggie Hui, the late Marilyn and the late Frank Hunt, Stephanye Hunter, Laura Inge, Marie Jena, Jillian Johnson, Knud Arne Jürgensen, Pria Karunaker, Maayan Keshet, Jock Ireland, Jillian Johnson, the Leslie Johnson family, Richard Kaye, Susan Kikuchi, Kim Kirschenbaum, Scott Klein, the late Sunil Kohtari, Rhona Koretzky, Richard Kornberg, Mindy Kristt, Lisa Labrado, Robert La Fosse, Kim Landsman, Natalie Lardner, Gavin Larsen, Simon Lauermann, William Lawson, the late Russell Lee, Ilyse Lefkowicz, David and Stacey Lehman, Laura Leivick, Wendy Lesser, the late Ellen Levene, Debra Levine, Jiani Liang, Janet and Irwin Light, the late Nancy Willard and the late Eric Lindbloom, David Lindner, Sheldon Lyke, Denise Machin, Alicia Graf Mack, Elizabeth Macklin, Deirdre MacMahon, Yvonne Marceau, Hadas Margulies, the late Gloria Marina (San Roman),

Sara Martucci, the late Katy Matheson, Charles (Chip) McGrath, Elizabeth McPherson, Mansi Mehta, Jodie Melnick, Kristen Miles, Martin and the late Sara Miller, the late Daniella Moffson, Eleanor Morris, Carina Moses, Stanley Moshman, William Murray, Moira North, Michael Novak, the late Patrick O'Connor, Eileen O'Malley, Daniel O'Neill, Miki Orihara, Tyna and Lowell Orren, Sena Oztosun, the late Aileen Passloff, Christopher Pennington, Francesca Perrone, Diane Pien, Robert Pierpont, Katha Pollitt, Robert Pontarelli, Kina Poon, Sam Prasad, Marianne Preger-Simon, Rajika Puri, Tashmin Rahman, Diana Rastagayeva, Gus Reed, Jack Reed, Hartmut Regitz, Teresa Reichlen, Susan Reiter, Carmen Ren, Jirina Ribbens, Jay Rogoff, Adria Rolnick, Ali Rosa-Salas, Jennifer Rosenthal, Meryl Rosofsky, Audrey Ross, Janice Ross, Andrew Rubenfeld, Deborah Rubin, Henning Rübsam, Sara Rudner, James Runsdorf, Kelly Ryan, Judith and Robert Samuels, Jonathan Schiff, Tracy Severe, Mr. and Mrs. Shukru, Marcia B. Siegel, Sharon Skeel, Jonathan Slaff, Jenna Smith, K. Mitchell Snow, Andrew Solomon, Wendy Ellis Somes, Jody Sperling, Evert Sprinchorn, Susan Stevens, Kaitlyn Sullivan, Kathryn Sullivan, Michelle Tabnick, TechtoUs, Anne Tobias, Tobi Tobias, Alexandra Tomalonis, Peter Townsend, Gary Tucker, Jorge Vargas, Myriam Varjacques, the late David Vaughan, Mansi Vira, Donna Wagner, Barbara (Bibs) Walker, Laura Webber, Meryl Weiss, Arnd Wesemann, Meryl Wheeler, Joe Williams, Adene and Richard Wilson, Robert Withers, Annie Wu, Billy Zavelson, Ellen Zeisler, Blake Zidell, John Ziv, Christopher Zunner.

Only the mistakes here belong entirely to me. Everything else connects.

This book was written in memory of my parents, my grandparents, and the following individuals: Rose Aloff Abramson, Dr. Manuel Album, Mildré Album, Abraham Aloff, Dinah Aloff, Edith Edwards, and Dr. Ida Jean Lee.

credits

index

about the author

Mindy Aloff is a writer and editor in New York City. She has published widely on cultural topics, dance a specialty, in periodicals and anthologies throughout the United States and in Europe and Japan. Some of her shorter articles and essays are archived on newyorkermagazine.com, nytimes.com, danceviewtimes.com, blog.bestamericanpoetry.com, and exploredance.com.

Featuring intriguing pairings of authors and subjects, each volume in the Why X Matters series presents a concise argument for the continuing relevance of an important idea.

Also in the series